And God Created Laughter

The Bible as Divine Comedy

Conrad Hyers

John Knox Press
ATLANTA

Library of Congress Cataloging-in-Publication Data

Hyers, M. Conrad.
    And God created laughter.

    Bibliography: p.
    Includes index.
    1. Wit and humor in the Bible. 2. Bible—
Criticism, interpretation, etc. I. Title.
BS680.W63H93   1987   220.6   86-46037
ISBN 0-8042-1653-3

© copyright John Knox Press 1987
10 9 8 7 6 5 4 3 2 1
Printed in the United States of America
John Knox Press
Atlanta, Georgia 30365

Acknowledgment is made for permission to reprint from the following sources:

To The Bodley Head and the Estate of Charles Chaplin for excerpt from Charles Chaplin, *My Autobiography* (New York: Simon & Schuster, 1964). Permission granted by The Bodley Head, 32 Bedford Square, London, W.C.1.

To The Bodley Head and the Estate of C. S. Lewis for excerpt from C. S. Lewis, *The Screwtape Letters* (New York: Macmillan, 1982) and *The Magician's Nephew* (New York: Macmillan, 1955). Permission granted by The Bodley Head, 32 Bedford Square, London, W.C.1.

To The Christian Century Foundation for material which originally appeared in *The Christian Century*, April 20, 1983, as "The Comic Vision in a Tragic World." Copyright 1983 Christian Century Foundation. Reprinted by permission from the 04/20/83 issue of *The Christian Century*.

To Fortress for excerpt from Walther Brondt, ed., *The Christian in Society*, II, © 1962 Muhlenberg Press. Used by permission of Fortress Press.

To Harper & Row Publishers for excerpt from William Barclay, *The Beatitudes and the Lord's Prayer for Everyman*, copyright 1963, 1964 by William Barclay. Permission granted by Harper & Row, Publishers, Inc.

To Macmillan for excerpt from George Bernard Shaw, *Saint Joan*, copyright 1924 by George Bernard Shaw. Permission granted by Macmillan.

To Pantheon for excerpt from Alan W. Watts, *Behold the Spirit: A Study in the Necessity of Mystical Religion*, copyright 1947 by Pantheon Books, Inc. Permission granted by Pantheon Books, a Division of Random House, Inc.

To *Presbyterian Survey* for permission to use and develop, in considerably revised and expanded form, materials that originally appeared in the *Presbyterian Survey*, April 1982, as "Easter Laughter," copyright 1982, Presbyterian Publishing House; and in *The Christian Century*, April 20, 1983, as "The Comic Vision in a Tragic World," copyright 1983, Christian Century Foundation.

To Princeton University Press for excerpt from Søren Kierkegaard, *Concluding Unscientific Postscript*, trans. David F. Swenson and Walter Lowrid. Copyright 1941, © 1969 renewed by Princeton University Press.

Preface

Special appreciation is due to Furman University, and to the Thomas F. Staley Foundation, for inviting me to deliver lectures at the University as a Staley Distinguished Christian Scholar. Some of the materials that now form this book, especially the Prologue, were developed in this context as a way of summarizing my interests in the function of laughter, humor, and comedy in the Bible.

Appreciation is also due to those in other places who have invited and attended addresses in which preliminary drafts of these chapters have been delivered: the National Clown, Mime, Dance, and Puppet Workshops in New York and Chicago; the United Ministries in Higher Education lecture series at Iowa State University; the Conference on Spirituality of the Presbytery of Three Rivers in Illinois; the Green Lake Baptist Assembly Family Conference in Wisconsin; the Clergy and Laity Retreat of the Episcopal Diocese of North Carolina; Christian Education Workshops of the Minnesota Valleys Presbytery; the Wellness Symposium of Mankato State University; the Peace Education Conference at Gustavus Adolphus College; the International Symposium on Reversal Theory at York University, Toronto; the Western Humor Conference in Phoenix, Arizona; and the World Humor Convention in Washington, D.C. The reception and encouragement of participants in these diverse settings have emboldened me to develop these materials more fully and to share them with a wider public.

The congregations of many churches in many states and of many denominations—Presbyterian, Lutheran, Methodist, Congregational, Baptist, Episcopal, Roman Catholic—will also recognize in these essays a sprinkling of anecdotes and themes that have been used in sermons and adult education classes. The Bible is a very nondenominational book, especially when interpreted in the spirit with which these materials have been given and received.

Department of Religion
Gustavus Adolphus College
St. Peter, MN

Contents

To the Memory of My Uncle

DAVID WESLEY SOPER
1910–1965
Professor, Preacher, Author

Whose Career Was
An Inspiration to My Youth

Prologue
Divining the Comedy

The Apostle Paul has a startling term for the Christian faith. He calls it *foolishness*. The cross is foolishness. Preaching is foolishness. God's work in the world is foolishness. The people through whom God works are noted for their foolishness. Christians are called to be "fools for Christ's sake." The apostles are ridiculed as fools, "a spectacle to the world, to angels and to men" (1 Cor. 4:9). Paul and his colleagues "have become, and are now, as the refuse of the world" (1 Cor. 4:13).

Paul had an unusual way of selling the gospel. His techniques have not been widely followed among either Jewish or Gentile merchants. Nor has he been hailed as a pioneer in the world of advertising. It is a wonder that the letter to the church at Corinth, which is introduced by such statements, has been preserved at all. It contains no appeals to human pride, no compliments for human achievement, no eulogies to human wisdom, no promises of economic and political gain, no worlds to conquer. Instead, insult is piled upon insult. Those whom God calls are said to be not only foolish but weak, low, despised, nothing, rubbish.

> God chose what is foolish in the world to shame the wise . . . what is weak in the world to shame the strong . . . what is low and despised in the world, even things that are not, to bring to nothing things that are. (1 Cor. 1: 27–28)

These remarkable passages in the early chapters of 1 Corinthians are, however, like a summation of the biblical message. The motifs of divine foolishness overturning human wisdom and of divine weakness overcoming human strength are threads that run throughout the Bible. This foolishness of God is come to "destroy the wisdom of the wise" and to thwart "the cleverness of the clever" (1:19). "Has not God made foolish the wisdom of the world? . . . For the foolishness of God is wiser than men, and the weakness of God is stronger than men" (1:20, 25).

Such themes form the plot lines of a good many biblical stories from Genesis through the Gospels and Acts. They are fundamental to the central biblical teachings from creation to Pentecost. They are familiar themes too, however, in the history of comedy. Paul, for example, would not have disliked the line from the eighteenth-century comedy *School for Scandal*: "We live in a very wicked world and the fewer we praise the better." Nor would he have disliked the way that comedy portrays and ridicules pride, gossip, hypocrisy, greed, slander, social cliques, vanity, and the like.

In comedy those who see themselves as wise are made to look foolish, and those who are foolish are found to have wisdom. Masters are treated as slaves, and slaves take the place of their masters. The hypocrisy of the self-righteous is exposed, and the virtues of rogues are revealed. Malicious gossips become the victims of their own malicious gossiping. The pretentious and the pompous are humiliated, and those whom they have humiliated are vindicated. The mercenary values of the rich and powerful are seen to be sordid; the simple values of the poor and humble are seen to be golden. Tyrants are deposed, beggars become kings, and the oppressed are set free.

Though the connection between biblical literature and comic literature is odd at first glance, in many important ways the Bible has sided with comedy, and, in turn, comedy has sided with the Bible. The following essays are an interpretation of biblical materials in terms of these comic themes. From this perspective the Bible takes on the appearance of a divine comedy. The major biblical stories use a similar pattern and offer a similar "moral" to many a comedy. In fact, the panorama of creation, revelation, and redemption witnesses to what might justly be called the humor of God.

In *The Comic Vision and the Christian Faith* I have offered an interpretation of the religious importance of the comic tradition.[1] That book focused on the wisdom of the fool, clown, jester, simpleton, underdog, humorist, comic hero, and trickster. Such figures function as the "prophets, priests, and sages" of comedy. They are the lead actors in an unfolding morality play that has remarkable affinities with biblical stories and teachings.

If that book looked at religious themes in the comic tradition, this book looks at comic themes in the biblical tradition. It is from this standpoint that many of the key biblical stories may be seen as closer to comedies than to any other type of literature. After all, the kingdom of God about which the Bible speaks is a kingdom that one enters, not like a king or at the right hand of a king, but on bended knee. The self-righteous are turned aside at the gate, and sinners are admitted instead. Children understand the way to this kingdom better than Jesus' own disciples. The poor, the meek, the merciful, and the persecuted are said to be blessed by the king of this kingdom.

When Jesus is asked for proof that he is the bringer of God's kingdom, he responds:

> . . . the blind receive their sight and the lame walk, lepers are cleansed and the deaf hear, and the dead are raised up, and the poor have good news preached to them. And blessed is he who takes no offense at me. (Matt. 11:5, 6)

The church has commonly interpreted this evidence of the presence of the kingdom of God in terms of miracles and powers. Yet why would anyone take offense at that? The real emphasis in Jesus' statement is upon the dregs and the derelicts of society who are being ministered to and brought into the kingdom—if need be on the sabbath: the blind, deaf, lame, leprous, dead, and poor. Surely the kingdom of Herod and the empire of Caesar were not organized along similar lines.

Comic devices are by no means foreign to the Bible. They are not always easy to see because of the enormous problems in trying to translate puns, plays upon words, ironic twists, satirical allusions. We usually miss the punch line and the point as well. As we say, it loses something in translation. Humorous expressions and the contexts that make them humorous are the most difficult items to convey from one language to another, even with cumbersome footnotes or parenthetical explanations—and once explained, they cease to be humorous anyway. Anyone who has learned a foreign language will appreciate the problems involved. The subtleties of humor are usually the last elements of a language that students are able to grasp. The tendency is to read everything in a very literal, one-dimensional manner—as we tend to read the Bible. Furthermore, oral humor cannot always be captured in a written account. How, for example, can one register in the words themselves whether the speaker was saying something tongue in cheek or smiling or laughing? Not a single wink makes its way to the printed page. Nevertheless, even in written form and in translation from Hebrew, Aramaic, and Greek, some examples do come through clearly. It is not difficult to imagine Jesus' hearers laughing heartily over the picture of a man with a log in his eye trying to take a speck of dust out of his brother's eye—and getting the point unforgettably.

Comic themes and devices are also not easily seen because of the prevailing assumption that such elements do not exist in Holy Scriptures. A person who is not open to the possibility of comic elements is not likely to be looking for instances or to see them, even by accident. The biblical writers, it is assumed, were a humorless lot. Most interpreters of Western comedy trace its roots back to Roman and Greek comedies, thus giving it a wholly Gentile, if not pagan, origin. The same assumption is made about satire or clowning or the fool. Everyone seems to know that the Jewish mind, throughout history, has been noted for its solemnity. One need only to consider Milton Berle, Art Buchwald, George Burns, and Woody Allen.

The God of Abraham, Isaac, and Jacob—and the God of Jesus and Paul—is also imagined to be totally humorless: infinite in gravity and without interest in children. The worshipers of this God, therefore, are presumably called to emulate such gravity. The suggestion is that the greater the degree of holiness, the lesser the degree of laughter and humor. Humor seems to be at the furthest remove from piety and propriety. It belongs in the streets but not the sanctuary, in the church kitchen but not in the church service. This understanding, however, serves better as a definition of sanctimoniousness and a pretext for fanaticism. How much evil is done in the world in the name of righteousness and rightness! And how much evil is ignored by ceremonialism! At best, humorlessness is more likely to qualify one for becoming a bishop than a saint, and even more likely, an inquisitor or an executioner.

It was an unfortunate omission on the part of the early church not to have included humor among the seven cardinal virtues and humorlessness among the seven deadly sins. The relationship between humor and virtues such as faith, hope, and love is much closer than has commonly been acknowledged. Where there is humor there is hope, and where there is hope there is humor. Persons whose faith and trust are in God, not just in themselves, are better able to have a sense of humor about themselves, their achievements, and their failures. Take the elderly Scottish Presbyterian woman who believed firmly in divine predestination and who, after falling down the stairs, got up, brushed herself off, and exclaimed, "Well, thank God that's over with!" That is faith *and* humor.

Even love is intimately related to humor. Consider the degree to which what is said of love in 1 Corinthians 13 could also be said of humor: "Love is patient and kind; love is not jealous or boastful; it is not arrogant or rude. Love does not insist on its own way; it is not irritable or resentful; it does not rejoice at wrong, but rejoices in the right. Love bears all things, believes all things, hopes all things, endures all things" (vss. 4–7).

This connection between humor and love, is anticipated in the medieval vision of Dante's *Divine Comedy*. In the *Commedia*, the residents of Hell (Inferno) are there because of self-love, which turns in upon the self as the center and goal of reality. They are imprisoned by the small, stifling world of selfishness. Each level in the descent into Hell is smaller than the preceding one, for self-love squeezes out others and concern for others. The result of pride, passion, and possessiveness is not an ever larger soul but an ever smaller soul. Those who are moving toward Paradise, however, are those who are turned outward, opening themselves to the divine love which is all-encompassing and therefore infinitely expansive and free. The movement through Purgatory to Paradise is one of a paradoxical enlargement of the soul through self-denial and self-giving.

When Dante entitled his work *Commedia*, he meant that it was written in "vulgar" Italian rather than classical Latin. Instead of the lofty and stately language of church, Scripture, and scholarship he chose the "lax and humble" language of home, street, and tavern—which was also the language of comedies. Dante meant, too, that his work moved from Hell to Heaven ("misery to felicity") and thus shared in the movement of many comedies from difficult straits to a light and happy ending. In a larger sense the term *commedia* is appropriate in that Dante's Hell is the least comic place—a point that was developed much later by C. S. Lewis in his epistles from Hell, *The Screwtape Letters*. Hell is the natural conclusion of self-love and thus of pride, greed, jealousy, lust, gluttony, and hatred. Self-love falls in upon itself, like the astronomer's black hole swallowing light. Heaven, on the other hand, is the most comic place. It is the highest level of the *Commedia*, for those who are there are the most open and free. They participate in a light and love that is all-embracing. As Dante exclaimed in approaching the eighth level of Heaven: "I seemed to see the Universe alight with a single smile" (Paradiso 27:4–5).

Some people have trouble with the word *comic* in a religious context. It immediately brings to mind comic books, most of which are not comic at all but bloodthirsty adventures. For others it brings to mind newspaper comic strips, the funnies, whose purpose is largely amusement and the solicitation of a laugh or two. Still others think in terms of stand-up comics and nightclub routines or the sitcoms that proliferate on the television screen. Terms such as *comic vision* and *comic spirit*, however, point to a certain perspective on life and an attitude toward life that are important to a full humanity. They belong both to the image of God in which we are created and to the image of Christ in which we are to be recreated.

There are also those who, on hearing the words *humor* and *comedy* associated with the Bible, suppose that the intent is to make fun of the Bible. If anything, it is the other way around. The Bible pokes fun at human pride and pretension, selfishness and greed, and the myriad other sins to which flesh and spirit are heir. Jesus freely used humor, irony, and satire to that end. His descriptions of the hypocrisies of the Pharisees use overtly humorous images: the blind leading the blind; straining out a gnat, then swallowing a camel; meticulously cleaning the outside of a cup while leaving the inside filthy; maintaining whitewashed tombs that are outwardly beautiful but inwardly full of dead bones; loudly honoring past prophets while plotting to kill present ones who preach the same message.[2]

Similarly, Isaiah made fun of the idol-makers of Babylon who would cut down a tree, carve a god out of one-half of the tree and roast meat over the other (Isa. 44: 14–17). Much earlier, Elijah had ridiculed the priests of Baal who wailed and slashed themselves in the frenzied hope that Baal would send fire from heaven. "Shout louder! . . . Perhaps he is deep in thought, or busy, or traveling; or perhaps he is sleeping and must be awakened!" (1 Kings 18:27, NIV). A more stinging satire was delivered by Amos against the rich and greedy wives of Samaria who pushed their husbands to gouge the poor more harshly so that they might indulge themselves:

> "Hear this word, you cows of Bashan,
>   who are in the mountain of Samaria,
> who oppress the poor, who crush the needy,
>   who say to their husbands, 'Bring, that we may drink!'
> The Lord GOD has sworn by his holiness
>   that, behold, the days are coming upon you,
> when they shall take you away with hooks,
>   even the last of you with fishhooks."
>
> (Amos 4:1–2)

In these and in other ways that will be explored in the following chapters, the Bible uses comic devices and themes to present a kind of divine comedy. The whole range of the comic—from gentle humor to biting satire—is employed. To appreciate this is to receive the gift of laughter and share in the humor of God.

There are always those who want terms defined, laboring under the assumption that the most complex issues can be pinned down by a few well-chosen phrases. Yet terms such as *humor*, *comedy*, *irony*, and *satire* are not easily compressed and packaged in this way.[3] They are best explained by description and example. Otherwise they too easily end up like the Sunday school child's definition of a lie: "A lie is an abomination before the Lord and an ever present help in time of trouble."

For the moment, an anecdote will suffice for identifying some of the marks of the comic spirit and perspective. It is from a story Robert Benchley tells of himself. While a student at Harvard University, Benchley was confronted with an examination question concerning a dispute between the United States and Great Britain over fishing rights and international waters. The students were asked to discuss the issues from the points of view of the two countries. Benchley wrote: "I know nothing about the point of view of Great Britain . . . and nothing about the point of view of the United States. Therefore, I shall discuss the question from the point of view of the fish!"[4]

In this case, the comic perspective is represented by the view of the fish. It is a viewpoint from which issues and situations are seen at an odd or unusual or unexpected angle. This is an angle that stands apart from the immediate circumstances and from conventional wisdom. It usually stands apart also from the parties in contention. To a worldly wisdom or to forces in conflict, the comic view often looks like foolishness. In this sense, however, the comic view is open to the possibility of representing a more godlike standpoint. Circumstances are placed in a larger perspective and seen from a more transcendent position. Even the viewpoint of the child or the fool or the fish may turn out to represent the viewpoint of God.

1

The
Humor
of
God

Sarah was childless. Month after month, year after year she waited for some sign of life stirring within her. To be without child was to be like a barren field. Decade followed decade, and the proud moment never came. Finally, in resignation, she offered Hagar, her maid, to Abraham that he might have an heir by her. Out of that union came Ishmael, "God hears," father of the Arabs. But jealousy and friction soon arose between Sarah and Hagar. Ishmael was a blessing for Abraham but not for Sarah.

Then one day when both Sarah and Abraham were very old, Abraham received a revelation that Sarah would bear him a son. On hearing this preposterous bit of news, Abraham fell to the ground in a fit of laughter. It was the most absurd joke he had heard in all of his ninety-nine years. When Sarah heard the news, she, too, laughed at such foolishness! God said, therefore, "you shall call his name Isaac"—that is, *laughter*.

A year later a son was born. "And Abraham called the name of his son . . . ['Laughter']! And Abraham circumcised his son ['Laughter'] when he was eight days old, as God had commanded him. Abraham was a hundred years old when his son ['Laughter'] was born to him" (Gen. 21:3–5).

The history of Israel begins—if it does not sound too impious—with a joke, a divine joke. The laughter of Abraham and Sarah at this joke was not so much a laughter of unbelief as of disbelief, as when we say "You can't be serious" or "You've got to be kidding." Yet it was a laughter that became the laughter of faith. Abraham and Sarah would be less inclined in the future to declare the impossible. And their laughter, in turn, would become the laughter of faith and hope for generations to follow.

The birth of any child brings a sense of the miraculous. That tiny bundle of human life evokes the sudden realization of the miracle of all life, including that particular life. Isaac, however, was a double miracle. Into this barrenness and hopelessness had come life and love and laughter. Upon his birth Sarah exclaimed in amazement and wonder: "God has made laughter for me; every one who hears will laugh over me" (Gen. 21:6).

The Foolishness of Sex

"God has made laughter for me." Isaac's birth is not the first creation of laughter, however. Laughter is the gift of creation, specifically of human creation. Though the creation stories of Genesis do not mention laughter as such, it is not foreign to the materials. In the story of Adam and Eve, Adam was created first, placed in a garden paradise, and given animal companions. Adam, nevertheless, was lonely. "What kind of paradise is this?" one can imagine him saying.

So God caused Adam to fall into a deep sleep, extracted from him a rib, and from it created a companion. She was "born" of Adam rather than from the ground (*adamah*), as was Adam, not so that Eve would be subordinate but so that she might be an equal. Taken from Adam's rib, Eve was unmistakably of the same order of being; for the animals, too, were created from the ground. When Adam awakened and saw one who was like himself, he exclaimed, "This at last is bone of my bones and flesh of my flesh" (Gen. 2:23). *The Living Bible* translates this in a livelier way by having Adam say more enthusiastically, "This is it!"

The creation of Eve was the creation of laughter. Into Adam's loneliness and incompleteness came life and love and laughter. He awakened suddenly to find someone standing there who was remarkably like, yet unlike, himself. Adam, too, exclaimed in effect: "God has made laughter for me." There now existed the laughter of companionship, of sharing and enjoying, of laughing together.

One can imagine in that encounter a great many other kinds of laughter: the laughter of surprise and astonishment at the unexpected ("Where did *you* come from?"); the laughter of incredulity ("I can't believe my eyes!"); the laughter of amazement ("It's a miracle!"); the laughter of discovery and recognition ("Is it really you?"); the laughter of suddenly seeing a reflection of himself but in another form ("You look like me, but somehow you're different"); the laughter of relief over a problem resolved ("At last, bone of my bone!"); the laughter of delight, joy, and celebration ("This is it!" or, as the English would say, "Super!").

Also present was the laughter that came from the new tension that had been created: the distinction between the sexes. Tension is a major source of laughter as a release mechanism, and the division of the whole human race into the male and female parts thereof has certainly been a major source of human tension, and therefore of laughter, ever since. Males and females are intrinsically odd to one another, and the "system" itself is very odd, no matter how accustomed to it we might become. Men have devised endless jokes about women, and women have humored themselves with stories about men. We have laughed together in companionship and sharing, but we have also laughed separately as a way of coping with differences and conflicts. In the words of an older love song, we are simultaneously "Bewitched, Bothered, and Bewildered" by the opposite sex. In this sense the creation of both Adam *and* Eve was the creation of laughter. It is the fundamental joke about the human race suddenly realized.

Implicit in this joke is the laughter that surrounds sexuality itself, whether male or female. Certainly the most ancient staples of comedy have been the earthen trinity of sex, food, and body wastes. In our self-consciousness and awareness of nakedness they become favorite topics of comic conversation. As W.C. Fields put it in *Tillie and Gus* (1933), "There comes a time in the life of every man when he must take the bull by the tail and squarely face the situation!"

With human existence a new arena of tension was opened up, one that animals do not experience and that Adam could not share with the animals. We are earthy creatures of the dust of the earth, Adam from *adamah*, flesh and bone among all creatures of flesh and bone. Yet, as the book of Ecclesiastes phrases it, God "has put eternity into man's mind" (3:11). We are suspended, as it were, between eternity and time, soul and body, thought and impulse, the infinite and the finite, incorruptible and corruptible, immortal and mortal. However that tension is to be phrased, and whatever such phrases may be said to mean or not to mean, it is a tension that is fundamental to human experience. It is not a fallen tension, but a tension within which we fall. Both reason and sex, rationality and passion, culture and nature, are aspects of the good creation. A requisite of our being as humans is that we take the bull by the horns and by the tail as well.

Genesis contains no hint that we have fallen into sexuality, as in the Platonic suggestion that humans were once like perfect spheres that have been split into male and female halves. Nor is there a hint in Genesis that an eternal soul has fallen into the quagmire of flesh, as in the Platonic view of the body as the prison house of the soul. The good creation is the creation of male and female who are both spirit and flesh. Out of these tensions we laugh, both in release and in celebration. In laughter we say that, for all of the awkwardnesses and perplexities of our being, the gods must be crazy but the gods must be good! The creation of sex and the sexes is a superlative example of divine foolishness.

Then, of course, laughter surrounds sexual union itself. "And they become one flesh" (Gen. 2:24). This is the laughter of intimacy—a point that the Eskimos have appreciated by referring to lovemaking as "laughing together." Adam and Eve delightedly explore the garden and each other. "Come, laugh with me." The most profound closeness with another comes through playfulness, including the playfulness of humor. When sex becomes deadly serious, it is performed either out of duty or out of lust. Only when there is playfulness, laughter, and good humor can there be true intimacy. The couple that plays together stays together! Freedom with one another does not come through taking oneself or the other only "seriously". One must take and be taken playfully, laughingly, humorously. In that way the awkwardness of male and female, spirit and flesh is transcended. It may even become graceful.

The Fall into Seriousness

All this is imaginable. In fact, within the measured words of the text, these dimensions are present implicitly, if not explicitly. Indeed, the best interpretation of these dimensions is still that of Mark Twain's *Eve's Diary*, not any of the thousands of commentaries offered by biblical scholars! The literal-minded interpreter, especially with little imagination and wearing the straitjacket of ultraseriousness, sees none of this. Literalism narrows meaning to exactly what is said and flattens it to its surface dimensions. As in trying to take a joke literally, the subtle nuances, the double meanings, the plays upon words—above all, the humor—get lost. To those who eliminate such possibilities from the start, no sense of play and laughter can be forthcoming at all. The literalist tends to approach the Bible with the grave assumption that such elements are not to be found in holy books or in the God who inspires holy books.

Some biblical interpreters also cannot wait to get on to the dark story of sin and the fall that follows the creation. Stories about evil and disaster, crime and punishment, seem more interesting than the suggestions that Adam and Eve amused themselves inside or outside Eden. We want to rush on to tales of forbidden fruit, murder, illicit sex, catastrophic floods, and fallen towers. How quickly theologians and biblical scholars pass over to this other shore and begin delivering interminable discourses on the fall, original sin, and general depravity! This hurry itself is one of the best arguments for the fall, and the continuing justification for the daily newspaper.

One would never guess from reading endless volumes of religious composition that humor has anything to do with God. The impression one gets is that God created *homo sapiens* but not the playful *homo ludens* or the good-humored *homo risens*. The only humanity that comes through clearly in the vast literature of religious thought is *homo gravis*.

The God of such religion is equally grave, if not supremely grave, on the theory that the Absolute must surely be characterized by absolute seriousness. If God created laughter, playfulness, and humor, few theologians, biblical scholars, or doctors of the church have ever heard about it. And if there is such a thing as the humor of God, it has never come through in our creeds, confessions, or catechisms. No wonder, for these are the things about which we endlessly quarrel.

There are, nevertheless, two sides to human existence. There is the side in which we are sober, serious, perhaps somber; and there is the side in which we are lighthearted, playful, smiling, laughing, joking, and maybe a little silly. Presumably we are both of these people, and presumably both define what it means to be fully human. Who wants to make sense or money all the time? Still, the almost overwhelming bias has been to associate God, religion, and humanity primarily with the serious side, preferably with our most serious moments. The lighter side is suspected of being a detraction from, if not a corruption of, a holy seriousness. Like the envious Salieri in Peter Schaffer's *Amadeus*, we don't know what to do with a Mozart who combines a divinely inspired music and high seriousness with raucous laughter and a love of foolishness. We see ourselves as most religious and reverential, if not a little godlike, when we are at our dreariest and dullest. We are uneasy about laughter and humor in the presence of God and the bishop. Laughter seems at the furthest remove from piety and faith while humor seems to imply a failure to take religion with a proper seriousness.

Reinhold Niebuhr, in the dark days at the end of World War II, wrote that laughter might be appropriate "in the vestibule of the temple, the echo of laughter in the temple itself, but only faith and prayer, and no laughter, in the holy of Holies."[1] Niebuhr wrote many wise things, but this is not one of them. His words reflect an old taboo, and one that goes right back to the garden. The fall is, if anything, the loss of laughter, not the loss of seriousness. Adam and Eve fell when they began to take themselves, their "deprivations," and their ambitions too seriously. And we have taken ourselves, our opinions and beliefs, our status and achievements, and our designs on the universe too seriously ever since.

The situation is not, as we have sometimes been led to believe, that laughter is the invention of the devil as a tool for engaging in frivolity and encouraging sacrilege, thus making children wiggle in church and giggle during confirmation. As Friedrich Nietzsche has suggested, it is the devil who is "serious, thorough, profound, solemn . . . the spirit of gravity—through him all things fall."[2] Laughter is fundamentally an act of celebrating existence. Laughter is an expression both of enjoyment and of thanksgiving. Thus laughter, humor, and comedy are commonly associated with feasting, parties, reunions, weddings, birthdays, spring rites—wherever people get together and say yes to life, in spite of its difficulties and its darker side.

Laughter is more than simply a necessary mechanism for dealing with the tensions and contradictions of fallenness. There is such a thing as fallen laughter, just as there is fallen reason and fallen sex. Fallen laughter is the kind we employ when we wish to ridicule someone or elevate ourselves above others. It is what racist jokes and sexist jokes and Polish jokes are made of. We laugh at and not with others. At its worst, fallen laughter can be malicious, cruel, sarcastic, mocking, arrogant, vulgar, bitter, and insane. The laughter of the crowd at Jesus' crucifixion was of this baser sort. Such laughter is a distortion of a gift of creation, which is basically good. As C. S. Lewis argued:

> Humor involves a sense of proportion and a power of seeing yourself from the outside. Whatever else we attribute to beings who sinned through pride, we must not attribute this. . . . We must picture Hell as a state where everyone is perpetually concerned about his own dignity and advancement, where everyone has a grievance, and where everyone lives the deadly serious passions of envy, self-importance and resentment.[3]

The Apostle Paul, when he was inclined to brag a little, boasted of his infirmities. This is the opposite of a fallen humor, in which one confesses one's worthiness and everyone else's unworthiness. Insofar as humor is not a celebration, it is properly a confession. Through humor we confess that we, too, like all other human beings, are finite, fallible, mortal, sinful, and frequently foolish. We confess that we "see through a glass, darkly," that "we know in part, and prophesy in part" (1 Cor. 13:12, 9, KJV). As a sixteenth-century comedy put it: "There are those with such profundities in their minds that, if you were to believe their writings, you would think they were God's first cousins!"[4] Apart from such reminders, piety is in constant danger of becoming pride, spirituality of turning into sanctimoniousness, and faith of falling into dogmatism and fanaticism.

Imago Dei

Through the ages considerable attention has been devoted to the question of what it means to be created in the image and likeness of God. Very little, however, has been said about laughter and humor as important aspects of the divine image or of the divine which that image supposedly reflects. Usually, nothing at all has been said. One could read through entire theological libraries and never guess such elements existed. When the subject of divinity is raised, even some hint of reflected divinity, the spirit of gravity immediately takes over. We begin to imagine a great many impressive features of the human personality: language, reason, conscience, imagination, creativity, aesthetic awareness, religiousness. We are not only *homo sapiens* but, as the new anthropology would have it, *homo sapiens sapiens*—doubly wise.

Although it is true that Genesis 1 does not mention laughter or humor as aspects of the image and likeness of God, neither does it mention any of these other attributes. The terms are used without elaboration. In the context, however, the basic concern of the creation account is with orderly relationships. How are all things properly situated relative to one another and to God? Where, in particular, are human beings to be located in the cosmic scheme of things? Humans were created on the same day as the land animals and are in many respects like them. Humans are also unlike the animals in being given dominion over the animals and the earth and granted a special relationship with God. Our likeness to God is thus the other side of our unlikeness to the animals. In the exuberant words of Psalm 8:4, 5:

> what is man that thou art mindful of him,
>   and the son of man that thou dost care for him?
> Yet thou hast made him little less than God,
>   and dost crown him with glory and honor.

This in-betweenness has almost invariably been interpreted in terms of the sober side of human existence, as if in this respect we were more like God and less like the animals. In so doing, of course, we have also affirmed that God is more like this side of human existence. The metaphor of work is seen as more appropriate for creation than the metaphor of play, and the image of gravity more appropriate for the creator than that of laughter. The resulting picture of "Nature, Humanity, and God" is essentially humorless.

Yet our humanity is characterized as much by playfulness as by work, by laughter as by seriousness, even by nonsense as well as sense. The ancient Greeks were not far from the truth in classifying human beings as "laughing animals." A fundamental difference between humans and donkeys, it was observed, was that donkeys can bray but only humans can laugh. If one has ever ventured to tell a joke, even the simplest of jokes, to one's dog or cat one senses the importance of the distinction. Animals take everything literally. They have no notion of double meaning, plays upon words, overstatement or understatement, incongruity or absurdity, irony or tongue in cheek. Animals also take everything quite seriously. They have some sense of play, but no sense of playing with their existence or with reality as such. Nor do they have the capacity to stand back from themselves and their situation enough to develop a sense of humor or a perception of the comical.

Tiger cubs can be very playful, but as the tiger matures this playfulness diminishes. Young baboons can be quite inquisitive and frolicsome, but old baboons become totally serious, all business and no nonsense. They cannot even effect a mock seriousness. Humans, however, have a capacity for playfulness that can be just as alive at age eighty as age eight. It may be more on the side of mind than body and of spirit than flesh, but it is thereby able to become more creative and enriching. Alfred North Whitehead, when he retired from an illustrious career in mathematics, took up philosophy and had an even more illustrious career to the age of eighty-six. The comedian George Burns at ninety may not have been able to move about as quickly as he did with Gracie Allen in his twenties and thirties, but the twinkle in his eye, the imagination, the playfulness and humor, were just as lively as ever. The person who is still able to wink can turn the entire universe upside down.

Quite bluntly put, seriousness we share with the animals; in laughter we laugh alone. The dog may wag his tail and the chimpanzee grimace and chatter, but only humans have the capacity for humorously playing with anything and everything, twisting things around, turning things inside out, inventing new things and reshuffling old ones. Nothing seems to stand outside our peculiarly human capacity for seeing all things from odd angles and for seeing the oddity in all things.

In C. S. Lewis' *The Chronicles of Narnia*, when Aslan creates talking animals, they discover laughter. At first they are ashamed by such "queer noises" and try to repress them. But Aslan says to them:

"Laugh and fear not, creatures. Now that you are no longer dumb and witless, you need not always be grave. For jokes as well as justice come in with speech."[5]

The Smile of God

Consider the child. For the first days of its life the infant just eats, sleeps, cries, and evacuates, with no clear evidence of its humanity. Despite assurances from everyone that the tiny creature looks remarkably like one or the other parent, it is a little animal. Then comes that magical moment in which the tiny face lights up and begins to smile. The smile is quite timid and quivering at first. The muscles have never been used in that peculiar way before. Yet one has the sense that whatever crying and gooing may have gone on before, in that smile the infant has given its first specifically human response. It has made the first step in joining the human race. Somehow in that hesitant and toothless smile, one has the feeling that one is looking into the face of God, that this has something to do with the image of God.

Well before the child evidences any of the more impressive characteristics of humanity—self-awareness, speech, abstraction—the child first of all smiles. Shortly thereafter comes laughter. Crying begins to be counterbalanced by laughter, and urgent desires for food and clean diapers by playful gurgling and exploring. The growing child learns to offset the weight of animal seriousness with a developing sense of humor, despite the fact that the adult world often encourages the former and discourages the latter.

William Wordsworth—for all his Platonism—was essentially correct in his "Recollections of Early Childhood":

> Not in entire forgetfulness,
> And not in utter nakedness,
> But trailing clouds of glory do we come
> From God, who is our home:
> Heaven lies about us in our infancy!
> Shades of the prison begin to close
> Upon the growing boy. . . .
> At length the Man perceives it die away
> And fade into the light of common day.

For the child, life is to be played, not worked at, and certainly not toiled at. Food is to be played with—as well as eaten—fingered, smeared, dumped, thrown, and gargled. Feet are to be played with, not just used for transportation. Life is to be lived playfully, laughingly, wonderingly. Soon, however, the worrying adult enters with a philosophy of all-seriousness and no-nonsense. The child must learn to laugh less and be serious more. One does not play at things; one works at them. The solemn and utilitarian mind begins to take over. What motivates learning is not fascination but a system of rewards and punishments and the future demands of the job market. Even games are no longer for fun. They are tests of skill, coordination, discipline. They are fueled by the desire to defeat an opponent. Sport is not for sport. It consists of *work*outs, the development of team*work*, and the preparation for one's life*work*. In short, children turn everything into play. Their parents turn play into work.

Parents are in a hurry to have their children grow up and get serious and are impatient with the carefree, playful world of the child. That world seems to go nowhere and accomplish nothing. For a child the most common adult questions are "Why don't you grow up?" and "Why don't you act your age?"—which is usually just what the child is doing. Such advice turns out to mean, "Why don't you become more like us?"—namely, nervous, worried, stiff, grouchy, irritable, bored!

Children have a secret. It is the secret of how to live. For all our dark sayings about original sin, children are still in touch with the garden of Eden. Most adults understand parenthood as an opportunity for children to learn from them. Yet the adult world is not all that it was made out to be as we were enticed along, emulating our seniors, unable to wait until we grew up, expecting all sorts of marvelous delights that would be available to us when we arrived in that promised land. Thus do we leave the land, flowing with milk and honey, and enter the land of the Philistines.

Parenthood might be better understood as an opportunity for adults to learn from children. It is true that children can be selfish and self-centered and short-tempered. They can be inconsiderate and impolite and messy. And they cry a lot—which is why children have to grow up. Still there are certain childlike graces that we tend to lose as we grow up, which is why adults need to turn and become once again like little children. True maturity does not come through killing and burying the children that we once were. In adolescence we imagine that maturity is achieved by escaping from that world and are mortified to be reminded of the children that we once were, knee-high to a grasshopper. Most of what passes for adulthood is really an advanced and hardened state of adolescence. True maturity involves a resurrection of childlikeness. As Joseph Campbell put it, "It is, in fact, only those who have failed, one way or another, [to preserve playfulness] in their manhood and womanhood, who become our penny-dreadfuls, our gorillas and baboons."[6]

Children have an irritating talent for not taking the adult world with the seriousness we are so confident it ought to be given. A refreshing air of innocent laughter blows like a gentle breeze from Eden through all the stuffiness of adulthood. With a persistent "Why?" or a completely candid remark, perhaps with a whimsical laugh or an unceremonious gesture, a little child can call into question the official façade and self-evident assumptions of an entire civilization. In the foolishness of the child there resides something of the wisdom of God. And in the laughter and playfulness with which children would instruct us there shines something of the face and image of God.

The Play of Creation

Nietzsche's Zarathustra said that he "should only believe in a God that would know how to dance."[7] He was never able to locate such a god, in part because in the history of biblical interpretation and theological discourse such possibilities had been so thoroughly obscured. Yet the God of the Bible is as much a God of the dance as of heavenly enthronement, of play as of work. We tend to look at Creator and creation in terms of six days of work and a seventh day of rest, but is this the only possible imagery? Certainly Psalm 104 is less methodical and more playful on the subject:

> O LORD, how manifold are thy works!
> In wisdom hast thou made them all;
> the earth is full of thy creatures.
> Yonder is the sea, great and wide,

> which teems with things innumerable,
> living things both small and great.
> There go the ships,
> and Leviathan which thou didst
> form to sport in it.
>
> (vss. 24–26)

For the psalmist the earth and sea teem with creatures whose profusion is as much for their own sake, like play, as for some larger purpose, like work. The objects of this creation have value in and of themselves; they are part of the goodness of creation. They do not have value simply in serving some grand design, some ulterior motive. Even Leviathan, that dread serpent of the sea, sports in the Mediterranean. The God of such creative prodigality is not merely hard at work, requiring a weekend of rest and relaxation after an exhaustion of energies. This God is one of whom it may be said: "Thou . . . coverest thyself with light as with a garment, who hast stretched out the heavens like a tent . . . who makest the clouds thy chariot" (Ps. 104:2, 3).

It is in creativity for the sake of creativity that human creation is most like the divine creation. Alan Watts once described the music of the great composers, such as Bach, as "pure play"—"a complex arrangement of glorious sounds, entirely sufficient in themselves." Their purpose was not extrinsic, such as making a living or pleasing the town council, but intrinsic—for the joy of it, for the fun of it.

> The intricate melodies flow on and on, and there never seems any necessity for them to stop. He [Bach] composed them in tremendous quantities, with the same Godlike extravagance to be found in the unnecessary vastness of nature. . . . Such playfulness is the very nature of the divine Wisdom.[8]

Only an inferior grade of music requires reasons and explanations for its existence. Perhaps this is why we speak of the works of great composers as divinely inspired, for in their creativity they reveal something of the divine playfulness in creation. On this scale the highest order of existence, both divine and human, is play. In play, things are not always turned into stepping-stones for getting elsewhere and achieving something else. Things exist and actions are performed for their own benefit. As in dancing, the object is not to reach some distant point on the dance floor, nor is it to arrive there as rapidly as possible. It is simply to enjoy the movements of the dance, which generally are circular and do not get anywhere at all and accomplish nothing beyond the act of dancing itself.

What, after all, is the point of Jupiter's twelve moons and Saturn's multiple rings or the craters pockmarking the moon? Why so many stars that no one could possibly count them, or even see them, let alone discern their significance? And why so much waste space in space? Always trying to make sense of the universe, to find purposes being worked out everywhere, discover plans being relentlessly pursued to exactly predestined specifications, perhaps even hear sermons in babbling brooks, is like Mark Twain's remarks about *Webster's Dictionary*: "This is a very interesting and useful book. . . . I have studied it often but I never could discover the plot."[9]

Can we look at the vastness of space, with its prodigious display of millions of galaxies and their billions of stars, its pulsars and quasars, comets and black holes, and not see God at play? Can we contemplate the swirling of spiral nebulae, or the gyrations of planets and their moons, or the spinning of electrons in their invisible orbits, and not sense the rhythms of a cosmic dance? Can we wonder about the number of other earths and unimagined life-forms a thousand light-years away in any direction and presume that such an unthinkable immensity leads only toward us and our miniscule fortunes? Can we survey the incredible zoo of creatures immediately before us or the countless creatures that have lived through the eons of time, leaving their fossilized traces and scattered bones as records of their momentary existence, and imagine our world to be simply serious business?

When we consider the millions of species of insects or the 150 million years of dinosaur remains or the profusion of plants that live or have lived from jungle to arctic, from ocean to mountain to primeval swamp, can we suppose that this explosion of life lies totally outside the comic domain? As one wit put it, "God *must* have a sense of humor; he created so many dinosaurs!"

Can we, then, witness the divine drama of revelation and salvation that the Bible unfolds in its patchwork of strange stories, meandering migrations, and roller-coaster fortunes of a people called Hebrews and not have the sensation of viewing a divine comedy? In the world of the Bible, too, we sense a superabundance of things great and small, mostly small. We are dragged through interminable genealogies, military roll calls, meticulous ceremonial codes, lists of petty kings, nuts-and-bolts inventories of tabernacles and temples, references to a host of inconsequential towns and people, and an array of trifling events and sundry tales. Often the amount of religious instruction, edifying discourse, and devotional liturgy is proportionately very sparse.

The Bible does contain an occasional mention of pharaohs and caesars, heroes and high priests. Yet the grand empires from Egypt to Rome appear like distant galaxies on the horizon, and the truly notable people are at best like faint stars on a moonlit night. Instead of moving forward resolutely with the main plot, the Bible gives the impression of being a kind of baroque novel where so much time is spent on minutiae and on the descriptions of minor characters that the reader gets lost every fourth page. To anyone who has undertaken to read the Bible straight through, the sensation is familiar. One has the feeling that one is playing the game of Trivial Pursuit or reading the ''Around Home'' section or the obituary column of a small-town newspaper.

Both the ''Book of God's Word'' and the ''Book of God's Works,'' as Francis Bacon phrased it, evoke the kind of reaction that a Mozart opera is said to have evoked in Emperor Joseph II: ''Too many notes.'' These observations are not intended to debunk the ''Book of Scripture'' or the ''Book of Nature.'' They point rather to some curious coincidences between these worlds and the world of comedy. The comic sense and the playfulness of humor seem to be more than simply idiosyncrasies of human achievement. The infant's smile and the laughter of little children, the humorist's jokes and the games people play, do not seem reducible to orphaned expressions of a humanity determined to make the best of an unresponsive universe that cares nothing for its hopes and fears.

This ''other side'' of human existence seems grounded in the nature of things and in the nature of the God who creates and sustains such an incredible phantasmagoria of space, time, and history. This other side corresponds as well to the strange world of the Bible which, for all its high seriousness, seems suggestive of a divine comedy. In all this are we not witnesses to the humor of God?

2

Easter
Hilarity

Euāngeliō (that we cal gospel) is a greke worde, and signyfyth good,
mery, glad and joyfull tydings, that maketh a mannes hert glad, and
maketh hym synge, daunce and leepe for joye.

—William Tyndale
Prologue to his English translation of the New Testament, 1526

Some time ago on "The Tonight Show," an Irish Catholic comedian
was remarking to a bemused Johnny Carson that the thing he appreciated most about the Catholic church is that the priest is called a "cele-
brant," whose office it is to "celebrate" the mass—except that he
never understood why, at some point in the ritual, the priest does not
break out of the rather funereal atmosphere and yell, "Whoopee!" The
suggestion has a sacrilegious ring to it, but not entirely. Though sin and
guilt, suffering and sorrow, death and injustice, are very real forces in
the world—in this case, Jesus himself being the victim—it is still legitimate to ask where the emphasis belongs.

In the early church the prevailing mood clearly was not funereal. It
was characterized by joy, celebration, praise, laughter. As Acts 2 indicates, the atmosphere was more that of a banquet or a victory party
than a memorial service for the dead. After Good Friday had come

Easter and Pentecost. Even the Lord's Supper, as much as its remembrance might seem to require somberness, seems in fact to have been celebrated, and in a banquet atmosphere. It had been placed in the context of the agape meal, the love feast, so that the bread and cup were lifted up and shared during a common supper. To be sure, things had gotten a little out of hand in Corinth, and the Apostle Paul had to issue a warning to that congregation about its excesses. Nevertheless, a banquet setting was seen as appropriate to what was understood as both a love feast and a victory feast (1 Cor. 11: 20–22).

> And day by day, attending the temple together and breaking bread in their homes, they partook of food with glad and generous hearts, praising God and having favor with all the people. (Acts 2:46–47)

The tragic remembrance of Jesus' broken body and shed blood was thus surrounded and uplifted by the joyful acceptance of them as the flesh and blood of God's self-sacrificing grace. The lament over Jesus' humiliation was transformed into the celebration of his self-emptying humility and self-giving love. Through his death, burial, and resurrection had come vindication and victory. In the words of Ecclesiastes, there was "a time to weep, and a time to laugh; a time to mourn, and a time to dance." Here, however, laughter and dancing came after weeping and mourning, and to them belonged the final note.

Freedom to Laugh

In the early Greek Orthodox tradition, an unusual custom developed along these lines. On the day after Easter, clergy and laity would gather in the sanctuary to tell stories, jokes, and anecdotes. The reason given was that this was the most fitting way of celebrating the big joke that God had pulled on Satan in the resurrection. A similar custom has been preserved in some rural Slavic areas where, on the day after Easter, folk dancing and feasting take place in the churchyard. In the early church, the "big joke" was also expressed humorously by representing Jesus as the bait in the mousetrap with which Satan was caught.

As frivolous as such post-Easter festivities might seem, they contain a very profound insight. What could be more appropriate to the day after Easter than laughter and gaiety reflecting the sense of liberation that comes through renewed faith in God's power and victory? If

Good Friday symbolizes sin and death and sorrow, it also symbolizes love and redemption. And Easter is the triumphant seal of that salvation: the recovery of life, the renewal of hope, and the laughter of rejoicing.

The German philosopher Nietzsche, in one of his several tirades against Christianity, declared that the Christian God is a tyrant, an oppressor, the enemy of life and the human spirit, a "spider" whose ensnaring web has to be broken in order that we might become fully human and fully free. But, to say the least, this is a curious statement in the light of the affirmation of the words attributed to Jesus in John's Gospel: "The thief comes only to steal and kill and destroy; I came that they may have life, and have it abundantly" (10:10). It certainly is clear that the early Christians saw themselves as liberated from oppression—the oppression of sin and fear, hopelessness and death. They had been set free, granted a new lease on life, and empowered by a new spirit. And in that spirit and freedom and fullness of life they rejoiced as those "filled with new wine" (Acts 2:13).

To be sure, some Christians have been killjoys, squeezing the life out of life by turning faith and trust in God into doctrinal rigidities and inflexible moral codes, as if faith and trust were essentially a matter of faith in our own rightness and trust in our own righteousness. And there are Christians who have been killjoys by identifying Christianity with a long face, stern countenance, and grave demeanor or the Christian spirit with a square-jawed, bulldog disposition, judgmental attitude, and militant temperament. The Lord's table has been turned into something resembling not only a funeral parlor but a debating society or an exclusive club. The good news of the gospel thus looks much like the bad news Nietzsche supposed it to be.

The situation sometimes is reminiscent of the position of the seventeenth-century Quaker Robert Barclay, who, in his *Apology for the True Christian Divinity (1676)*, insisted that Christians should shun everything that does not suggest the utmost seriousness, gravity, sobriety, and fear of God. "For laughing, sporting, gaming, mocking, jesting, vain talking, &., is not Christian liberty, nor harmless mirth."[1] According to such a definition, a truly "divine" Christian ought to look something like a cross between a sour lemon and a dried prune. But this is hardly an accurate image of that spirit of "love, joy, peace, and long-suffering" that comes to those whose confidence and hope is in God and not in themselves—not even in their own piety and propriety.

In the Christian liberty of the gospel, we are liberated from, among other things, the awesome responsibility for gaining infallible truth and possessing the final knowledge of good and evil, which belong only to God. We are accepted not only in spite of our sinfulness but in spite of our finiteness and fallibility and foolishness. We are justified neither by goodness of works (as the Reformers so clearly pointed out) nor by correctness of belief (as they did *not* so clearly point out) but by the free gift of divine grace. If we are not saved by our own righteousness, neither are we saved by our own rightness. Those who live in grace are freed from the necessity of taking themselves, their circumstances, their morality and opinions, their piety and beliefs, too seriously. They are free to laugh and play as children of God.

The relationship between faith and humor is an intimate one. On the one side is the peril of idolatry and pride. On the other side is the peril of unbelief and despair. Faith without humor becomes fanaticism; humor without faith becomes cynicism. Religious experience and expression at their best, therefore, exist in a delicate balance between faith and laughter.

The taboo surrounding the comic spirit is a venerable one in the history of the church. In the year 390 Chrysostom preached a sermon against laughter and playfulness, which he saw as too close to paganism and too far from Christian decorum and devotion. "This world," he proclaimed, "is not a theatre, in which we can laugh; and we are not assembled together in order to burst into peals of laughter, but to weep for our sins. . . . It is not God who gives us the chance to play, but the devil."[2]

Such a position, however, is in danger of being more supportive of paganism than the Bible. As important as repentance may be, we are not saved by our much weeping, any more than we are saved by acts of penitence. And the expression of salvation freely given and received is not weeping but laughter, or at least a weeping become laughter. Thus, to reverse the words of Chrysostom, it is not the devil who gives us the chance to play, but God. Laughter and lightheartedness, at their fullest and freest, are not pagan possibilities but the gift of divine grace.

There are psalms, of course, that cry out in confession and repentance: "Have mercy on me, O God, according to thy steadfast love" (Ps. 51:1). And there are psalms that cry out in lamentation over misfortunes and illnesses and sufferings: "My God, my God, why hast thou forsaken me?" (Ps. 22:1). These expressions are an important part of the "time to weep" and the "time to mourn" of Ecclesiastes.

Yet many psalms, the preponderance of psalms, can hardly be classified as solemn and sobering; indeed, the word *psalm* is nearly synonymous with praise. "I will bless the LORD at all times; his praise shall continually be in my mouth. . . . Look to him and be radiant" (Ps. 34:1, 5). The whole range of human emotion is represented in the psalms. Of this range, the fundamental mood is that of rejoicing, thanksgiving, celebration. "Blessed is the man who. . . . Praise the LORD!" These are the first and last words of the psalmody, the alpha and the omega of biblical expression. The mood is that of the first and last books of the Bible itself, beginning in Genesis with a hymn of praise to the Creator and culminating in Revelation with a vision of hope in a new heaven and a new earth. In between are other, darker moods and expressions. But they are secondary, not primary.

The Comic Parenthesis

Similarly, in the Gospels, Jesus' ministry begins and ends in celebration. It is quite remarkable that Jesus is not pictured as beginning his work with a sermon or a healing or even a theological debate with the Pharisees, but with a marriage feast. We might expect such a beginning to be beneath the dignity and serious purpose of Jesus' ministry, one that the disciples might have conveniently forgotten to mention. Yet it is recorded by John as having special introductory significance. Immediately after Jesus' temptation in the wilderness, his baptism, and those weighty pronouncements by John the Baptist that Jesus is the Messiah and the Lamb of God, what is the first act of his ministry? Jesus goes off to Cana of Galilee and takes what looks like a week's vacation at a marriage feast—which in that time lasted several days. We have no indication that Jesus went to the wedding festivities to preach or teach or moralize; he went simply to share in the celebration. Furthermore, the culminating act of the feast was Jesus' turning six jars of water into wine, "each holding twenty or thirty gallons," and it was said to be the best wine of the feast (John 2:6).

One's initial reaction to this first miracle (particularly after centuries of pious evangelical efforts to turn that wine back into water) is to ask, What kind of Messiah is this? Is this an example of the "Father's business," which the twelve-year-old Jesus said he needed to be about? Perhaps it was this puzzling beginning, along with subsequent rumors that Jesus was eating and drinking with publicans and sinners, that later led the imprisoned John the Baptist to have second thoughts about his grand pronouncements concerning the person of Jesus. Did not John send his disciples to Jesus with the question, "Are you he who is to come, or shall we look for another?" (Matt. 11:3).

An important contrast is hidden in this exchange, to which Jesus himself calls attention. "John," he says, "came neither eating nor drinking, and they say, 'He has a demon'; the Son of man came eating and drinking, and they say, 'Behold, a glutton and a drunkard, a friend of tax collectors and sinners!' " (Matt. 11:18–19). Of course, Jesus was not a glutton and a drunkard, but neither was he a John the Baptist. John's life was one of severity and renunciation: living in the wilderness, wearing camel's hair, eating locusts and wild honey, and preaching judgment and repentance. Jesus, on the other hand, left the wilderness for the cities and villages of Palestine, ate with publicans and sinners, befriended women of doubtful repute, challenged those who were quick to judge others and to throw the first stone, and preached a message of forgiving love and redeeming grace.

Not surprisingly, the disciples of John also came to Jesus on another occasion to ask, "Why do we and the Pharisees fast, but your disciples do not fast?" To this Jesus responded, "Can the wedding guests mourn as long as the bridegroom is with them?" (Matt. 9:15). If John the Baptist represented the death of the old era in preparation for the new, Jesus represented the birth of the new in which all might "have life, and have it abundantly" (John 10:10). Yet, strangely, the church has tended to mold Jesus in the image of John the Baptist! Christians have often been more adept at looking and behaving like disciples of John than of Jesus.

The image of Jesus throughout most of the history of Christian art has been that of the serious, somber, or suffering Jesus. Sometimes it has been the gentle Jesus, meek and mild, or the kindly Jesus flocked by children, or the shepherd Jesus tenderly carrying a lamb in his arms. And, of course, there are the myriad portrayals of the infant Jesus, bambino of so many nativity and early childhood scenes. The central image, though, is the crucified Jesus, whose expressions range from forlorn resignation to tortured agony. The identification is strongly, almost overwhelmingly, on the side of weeping and mourning. Insofar as the image transcends what otherwise would be the stark portrayal of death, defeat, and hopelessness, it conveys an equally heavy sense of divine solemnity and messianic freight.

The crucified Lord who walks the Via Dolorosa and who cries out, "My God, my God, why hast thou forsaken me?" is certainly and legitimately central to Christian sentiment and imagination. Still, this image represents neither the first nor the last word. Jesus' ministry begins with the festival atmosphere of the marriage feast of Cana and ends with the festival atmosphere of Easter and the post-Easter appearances. More broadly, it begins with the joyful annunciation to Mary and the angelic allelulias heralding Jesus' birth, and it ends with the ascension and the birth of the church on Pentecost.

This is the grand parenthesis within which Jesus' ministry takes place. In between are disappointment, rejection, conflict, sorrow, suffering, and death. In between are Gethsemane and Golgotha. Yet the overarching context remains one of celebration and joy, of life and love and laughter. Jesus may be the sacrificial lamb, slain for and by the sins of the world. But it is important to know who is making the sacrifice and giving the feast. The first and the last words belong not to death but life, not to sorrow but joy, not to weeping but laughter.

This is the parenthesis in which we, too, are called to live. The life of the Christian is not lived in the context of Good Friday and crucifixion, but in the context of Easter and Pentecost. Although our lives also are subject to tragedy and heartache, we live not in the time of doubt and hopelessness and despair, but of faith, hope, and trust. We live in the time of the love feast of the church and the marriage feast of the bride of Christ. And although we are no more exempt than others, or than Jesus himself, from the hard and harsh side of life—and there is therefore a time for weeping and mourning—there also is a time to laugh and a time to dance. The final expression belongs to dancing and laughter. Even "death is swallowed up in victory" (1 Cor. 15:54).

In one of Aldous Huxley's early novels there is a character who, upon being converted to Roman Catholicism, promptly gains weight and begins to compose a book of humorous verses about the crucifixion. Whether these might be accepted by ecclesiastical authority as the most desirable evidences of conversion, they do reveal a sense of liberation and suggest an air of celebration.

The Scaffold that Sways the Future

Paul speaks not only of the "foolishness of the cross" but of the foolishness of preaching about the cross. Certainly the suggestion that Jesus' death was anything but the good riddance of a troublesome agitator, disturber of both Jewish and Roman peace, looked like foolishness both to Jew and to Gentile. The very idea that this homeless, jobless, and powerless man, with no political aspiration and no economic or military base, was a serious threat to the house of Herod, let alone the house of Caesar, was preposterous. Or the claim that this itinerant preacher, elected by his own people to be crucified instead of Barabbas and forsaken by his own closest followers, was of great significance in human history must have seemed like total nonsense—"a stumbling block to Jews and folly to Gentiles" (1 Cor. 1:23).

No doubt people thought that day on the hill of Golgotha that his death was the end of the matter, that his voice had been silenced and his influence shattered. Even his own disciples went back to their fishing nets. Yet it was this cross and this humiliation that became for ever-increasing numbers a symbol of victory not of defeat, of hope not of despair, of love not hate. The weakness of God proved stronger than the strength of men. As it turned out, it was not the chief priest or Herod or Pilate but the crucified Christ who was to become a mighty force in history. In the words of a familiar hymn, "Once to Every Man and Nation," adapted from James Russell Lowell:

> Though the cause of evil prosper,
> Yet 'tis truth alone is strong,
> Though her portion be the scaffold,

And upon the throne be wrong,
Yet that scaffold sways the future. . . .

The nineteenth-century Danish writer, Sóren Kierkegaard, had another term for Christian teaching. He called it "Absurd." By this he did not intend to dismiss the teaching but rather to insist that it represents a kind of religious truth that lies beyond the easy access of human reason. Conventional wisdom is unable to comprehend it or add it to the collection of assured truths. The absurdity of God present in the flesh—the infinite in the finite—and the contradiction of the victorious victim confounds the cleverness of the scribe and the debater of the age.

There are, however, *tragic* absurdities and *comic* absurdities. Tragic absurdities lead to destructive consequences. It is absurd that Sophocles' King Oedipus, by the strange twists and unhappy coincidences of fate, should unwittingly kill his father and marry his mother. Such a tragic absurdity brings his once happy world crashing down around him, and he is left in blindness and despair. Though we may be inspired by and find consolation in the noble way in which King Oedipus submits to his absurd fate (the so-called tragic catharsis), there is nothing redemptive about the revelation of this absurdity. The news is devastating.

Comic absurdities, on the other hand, lead to constructive consequences. Most immediately a comic absurdity issues in laughter and enjoyment, as in the sudden absurdity in the punch line of a joke. More largely, a comic absurdity is the coming together of two highly improbable, seemingly impossible, and certainly surprising opposites. Such a coming together, however, is not a tragic collision of forces, culminating in death and destruction. Rather it is a coming together of opposites on their way to a happy conclusion. Forces previously alienated or at odds are brought into harmony. A chaotic situation becomes orderly. A broken condition is healed. Comic absurdities thus are redemptive. They issue in reconciliation, unity, wholeness, and celebration.

In these terms, the Christian message begins in a comic absurdity: the bridging of the divine and the human, the juxtaposition of the royal son born in an animal shed, the visitation both by Jewish shepherds and Gentile magi. As the story unfolds, however, it moves toward what seems to be a tragic end. Jesus, while shunning power and worldly gain, is caught between conflicting forces: Jew and Gentile, imperialist and nationalist, and rival religious leaderships within Israel. As often happens, those who would stand apart from opposing sides or who would mediate between them, end up the target of both sides. Jesus, though rejecting the kingdoms of the world, is crushed between contending kingdoms.

With Easter, however, the story switches from a tragic to a comic absurdity. The victim is victorious, even though the powers that be remain in apparent full sway. "O death, where is thy victory? O death, where is thy sting?" (1 Cor. 15:55). The mood is suddenly and radically transformed from the mood of Good Friday so that it may indeed be called *Good* Friday. The scene is dramatically reversed. The story results not in alienation but resolution, not in weeping but laughter, not in mourning but dancing. In Northrop Frye's words: "tragedy is an episode in that larger scheme of redemption and resurrection to which Dante gave the name of *commedia*."[3]

Spring Rites

There is a further intriguing parallelism of tragedy and comedy. Early in this century Francis Cornford advanced the thesis that the origins of both tragedy and comedy are to be found in the ancient Greek spring rites.[4] The first movement of these rites portrayed the death of the old year and of the king, and thus a return to chaos and infertility. Out of this movement, suggested Cornford, came some of the themes of Greek tragedy. Tragic action belongs to winter. Life and the struggle of life lead eventually to conflict, death, and disorder.

The second half of the spring rites, however, moved in an opposite direction. New life began to burst forth. The dead king was resurrected or replaced by a young king. A new kingdom and a new order were instituted, with a recoronation and a renewal of allegiance. There was a marriage of the king, a gala procession and a wedding feast, the marital union ensuring ongoing abundance of life. Out of this movement, suggested Cornford, came Greek comedy. Comedy belongs to spring. In comedy, suffering and death lead to life and renewal. Comic action culminates in parades, weddings, and feasts.

The Christian drama of Holy Week follows a remarkably similar pattern, moving at first in a decidedly tragic direction. On Palm Sunday, Jesus is hailed as king in the lineage of David, then crucified as a mock king. He is dressed in the purple robe of royalty, given a crown of thorns, and ridiculed as a fool's king both by the crowds and by the placard placed above his head—"King of the Jews." Even his disciples deny him or follow him from afar. Ominous darkness descends upon the landscape as he dies the slow, agonizing death of the cross. He is buried in a stranger's tomb, and his disciples scatter, dejected and disillusioned. Seemingly faith, hope, and love have been conquered by the forces of hatred, unbelief, and tyranny. Thus far the story seems thoroughly tragic.

Yet the tragic action is not given the last act or the final scene. As in the ritual drama of the spring rites, the descent is followed by an ascent. After death comes resurrection and a renewal of faith and hope. The seed of the kingdom of God, small as a mustard seed, must fall to the earth and die in order to bring new life. The church that emerges from the apparent ashes of former discipleship now understands itself as the bride of Christ. Its humble beginnings are the inception of a new kingdom and a new order. The Last Supper, instead of being read only in the tragic mode as the dark foreboding of Gethsemane and Golgotha, is also read in the comic mode as a celebration of that "living bread which came down from heaven." The broken body and shed blood represent death, to be sure, but also life. "If any one eats of this bread, he will live for ever; and the bread which I shall give for the life of the world is my flesh" (John 6:51).

Thus, paradoxical though it may seem, the remembrance of Christ's broken body and shed blood was not conducted in the early church after the fashion of a funeral service or a war memorial to the fallen dead. It was more like a thanksgiving, a celebration. The mood was jubilant and triumphant. Finally we must ask, as Wylie Sypher has put it, whether "the drama of the struggle, death, and rising—Gethsemane, Calvary, and Easter—actually belongs in the comic rather than the tragic domain."[5]

This does not mean, however, that the comic mood is simply a matter of celebrating happy endings, either now or hereafter. The comic spirit does not depend wholly upon everything turning out all right; nor does it derive its buoyancy solely from that blissful prospect. Most interpreters who have noted connections between biblical scenarios and theatrical comedy have made this mistake.[6] If a comedy is defined primarily by some final scene of triumph, love, and harmony, there is no clear difference between a comedy and a romance or a fairy tale. In a romance the hero, working against terrible odds, is victorious both in love and in war. In a fairy tale a prince who has been turned into a frog by a wicked witch is released by a maiden's kiss, and they wed and live happily ever after.

Even if many comedies do end similarly, the spirit is not the same. In a romance or a fairy tale the suggestion is that one could only be happy if life could be lived "happily ever after." The romance or fairy tale has no capacity for living happily in less than ideal circumstances and no suggestion at all as to how to live in the midst of very difficult circumstances. Yet the uniqueness of comedy is the way in which life is lived, regardless of the immediate circumstances. Comic heroes are defined by an ability to cope with life's lows as well as highs, in large part because they have considerable flexibility and are not trapped by an absolute seriousness. They represent a spirit that is determined to introduce playfulness, lightheartedness, and laughter into life as a whole. They therefore exemplify a resiliency of spirit that may be down but never out. They are able to celebrate life not only when everything is coming up roses but when everything is coming up dandelions, or perhaps coming up with nothing at all.

In Everything Give Thanks

It is here, in the midst of darkness and difficulty, not just among the lilies of an Easter ending, that the Christian spirit has much in common with the spirit toward which comedy is aiming. The Apostle Paul certainly eulogizes and theologizes about the resurrection, sometimes at length, as in 1 Corinthians 15. Yet Paul does so in the midst of the real world of the Roman Empire under Nero, not as one who has just heard the words "today you will be with me in Paradise" (Luke 23:43). Paul furthermore, since his conversion to Christianity, has hardly had happy circumstances. In fact, he has had considerable trouble ever since:

Five times I have received at the hands of the Jews the forty lashes less one. Three times I have been beaten with rods; once I was stoned. Three times I have been shipwrecked; a night and a day I have been adrift at sea; on frequent journeys, in danger from rivers, danger from robbers, danger from my own people, danger from Gentiles, danger in the city, danger in the wilderness, danger at sea, danger from false brethren; in toil and hardship, through many a sleepless night, in hunger and thirst, often without food, in cold and exposure. (2 Cor. 11:24–27)

Paul is not exactly describing heaven or ecstasy or even a church picnic. We might well expect him to have concluded from all this that he had made a wrong turn somewhere on the road to Damascus. Certainly we expect this catalog of tortures to lead to a cry of injustice and a bitter complaint against heaven. Yet, no, the response is that of remarkable acceptance and equanimity: "I am content with weaknesses, insults, hardships, persecutions, and calamities; for when I am weak, then I am strong" (2 Cor. 12:10). Or, as he writes to the church at Philippi: "I have learned, in whatever state I am, to be content. I know how to be abased, and I know how to abound; in any and all circumstances I have learned the secret of facing plenty and hunger, abundance and want. I can do all things in him who strengthens me" (Phil. 4:11–13).

As in many comedies what is often tested is not the capacity to celebrate when the banquet table is full or the wedding consummated or the victory achieved. That kind of celebration comes easily enough and requires no special fortitude or encouragement. Instead, the question raised is whether it is possible to celebrate life when the sky is not blue and fortune is smiling less broadly upon us. Most of the materials that comedies work with are the everyday problems, tensions, anxieties, mistakes, conflicts, failures, and annoyances that make up so much of our lives and that usually have us nervous, outraged, in tears, or tearing our hair out. Yet through the comic perspective these are the very things that we now stand back and laugh about. We celebrate the life given to us in spite of, and to some extent even because of, its hard and harsh side. If there were a comic prayer, it would probably go something like this: "O God, though we do not live in the garden of Eden, we are nevertheless still glad to be here."

In this sense, it is not just the triumphant ending of Holy Week that is comic or the eschatological ending of the New Jerusalem and a new

heaven and earth. The present moment is placed within a comic parenthesis and lived out of a comic spirit. As Paul advises the church at
Thessalonica, "Rejoice always . . . give thanks in all circumstances"
(1 Thess. 5:16, 18). Such advice comes across as foolishness to a
worldly wisdom that would advise blessing the good and cursing the
evil, being thankful for the best of times and complaining about the
rest. Yet there it is in all its boldness and foolhardiness. Paul also de-
scribes such a spirit to the Ephesians: "always and for everything giving thanks" (5:20). After all, regardless of how glorious the end might
be, the present moment is the moment we have been given and in
which we must live. The immediate issue is the spirit in which we are
to live *this* moment, whatever the circumstances or outcome.

From this standpoint a figure such as Job is to be admired, not because after losing everything he is eventually given "twice as much as
he had before" (Job 42:10) but because of the response he gives upon
losing everything: "The LORD gave, and the LORD has taken away;
blessed be the name of the LORD" (1:21). There are those who have
attempted to classify Job as a comedy because "the LORD blessed the
latter days of Job more than his beginning; and he had fourteen thousand sheep, six thousand camels, a thousand yoke of oxen, and a thousand she-asses"—exactly double the number he had lost (42:12).[7] Yet
the real test of the spirit of Job is to be found amid the losses themselves, when his wife urges him to "curse God, and die" and Job responds, "Shall we receive good at the hand of God, and shall we not
receive evil?" (2:9–10).

In one of Chaplin's early comedies, *The Tramp* (1915), he introduced what appeared to be the opposite of the traditional comic ending.
As the film begins, the tramp is walking down a dirt road, jobless and
friendless and homeless. He chances upon a farmer's daughter on her
way to shop in the village, being set upon by three thieves. By trickery
and luck he rescues the "damsel in distress," and in gratitude she takes
him home to meet her father. The father invites him to dinner and offers him a job as a reward. For a time a love affair seems in the making, along with a new future as a farmhand. Then the daughter's dapper
boyfriend from the city drives up. She completely forgets Charlie, and
when he sees them embracing he realizes that her affection was only
gratitude and kindness. Dejected, he scrawls a farewell note on a scrap

of paper. As he trudges sadly away, he is offered some money by the city beau, which he refuses. Head down and shoulders stooped, he walks slowly back down the same dusty road by which he entered the scene. Again he is jobless, friendless, and homeless.

Then in the final frames a transformation occurs. Suddenly he stands erect, kicks up his heels, shakes off the dejection, and walks briskly away with a jaunty gait. He refuses to let the failures and disappointments of life have the victory. He picks himself up, dusts himself off, and regains his balance, his freedom, and his good cheer. This is the comic triumph. The Tramp is determined, in whatever state, to be content.

Such is the spirit captured so well in Ella Wheeler Wilcox's poem about sailboats:

> One ship drives east and another drives west
>   With the selfsame winds that blow.
>   'Tis the set of the sails
>   And not the gales
> Which tells us the way to go.
>
> Like the winds of the sea are the ways of fate,
>   As we voyage along through life:
>   'Tis the set of a soul
>   That decides its goal,
> And not the calm or the strife.
>
> "The Winds of Fate"

3

A
Chosen
People
of
God
Contest

One of the favorite anecdotes told of Abraham Lincoln concerns an eight-year-old girl who wrote to him suggesting that he grow a beard. In her opinion, the letter said, Lincoln would stand a better chance of election if he would grow a beard to hide his homely face. With some people of importance such a letter would not have stood a chance. Yet not only did Lincoln answer her letter personally, he thanked her for her suggestion. He further added that should his campaign be coming in her vicinity, he hoped he would have the opportunity to meet her and to express his appreciation personally.

A television comedy of the 1970s, *"The President's Whiskers,"* picked up on the story. Though the incident was considerably embellished, the dramatization was true to the spirit of the story. It captured the magnanimous sense of humor that was part of Lincoln's greatness as well as the delightful comedy implicit in the anecdote itself. Others, more concerned about status and less inclined to take advice from small girls, might have considered the letter a personal affront; Lincoln took the counsel with grace and good humor.

The story illustrates well the gentle humor and high comedy to be found in the Bible. In the television version the letter from Lincoln spurred a flurry of activity in the girl's town, where her father was a

member of the local Republican party. On learning of the letter the officials of the party were ecstatic at the prospect of a visit from Lincoln.
They saw visions of political prestige, special favors, positions in
Washington, perhaps even a cabinet post. Introductions were prepared,
speeches written, a band rehearsed.

On the day that Lincoln's campaign train was scheduled to pass
through the town, practically the whole town was assembled at the sta-
tion. There were the leaders of the Republican party, the local officials
wearing their top hats, the shiny marching band, the ladies and gentlemen and schoolchildren in their finest attire. Almost everyone was
there, that is, but the little girl to whom Lincoln had written. She had
been left home with the black maid and her daughter. Lincoln, of
course, would be interested only in the politicians and their speeches,
and the voters and their votes, not the attentions of little girls.

It so happened, however, that as the campaign train approached the
town, it was forced to stop for repairs. Lincoln, not wanting to sit in
the warm train, set off across the fields on foot. Walking through the
streets of the empty town, he found an elderly man who gave him directions to the little girl's house. When Lincoln introduced himself at
the door, the black maid was speechless. But the little girl and her
black playmate welcomed him in with the complete lack of bowing and
scraping known only among young children.

The two girls had been having a pretend party, drinking pretend hot
chocolate out of small teacups. Naturally, they invited Mr. Lincoln to
join them and "poured" him a cup. In the marvelous scene that follows, Lincoln is sitting in the parlor with the two little girls, engaging
in their small talk and sipping pretend hot chocolate with them. After a
while, Lincoln says he must be going, thanks them for the party and
the hot chocolate, and asks them how they like his new beard. Then he
walks back across the field to the waiting train.

The final scene is priceless. Lincoln's campaign train goes right
through the town without stopping! It goes right past all the waiting
politicians and local dignitaries; right past the loud-playing band and
the flag-draped platform; right past the ladies and gentlemen in their
Sunday best. For Lincoln had just come to visit and say thank-you to
an eight-year-old girl.

Biblical Heroes

However apocryphal this version of the story, it is characteristic of
the type of comedy that has some rather remarkable affinities with the
biblical message. We do not usually associate the word *comedy* with
the Bible. Yet a common concern in comedy and the Bible is human
pride and pretension. Both deal with the arrogances of power and status
and the follies of selfishness and self-importance. Jesus' terse comment
that "whoever exalts himself will be humbled, and whoever humbles
himself will be exalted" (Matt. 23:12) is not only a fundamental biblical theme but a fundamental theme in the history of comedy. A standard comic device is for the braggart to be humiliated and the underling
vindicated. The high and mighty have a great fall, and the lowly and
downtrodden are elevated in their stead.

The structure of many biblical stories is much the same as a comedy like *"The President's Whiskers."* The words from the Magnificat
of Mary could easily be used as a summation of the comedy: "He has
filled the hungry with good things, and the rich he has sent empty
away" (Luke 1:53). So characteristic is this theme in both comedy and
the Bible that the term *divine comedy* is really as appropriate as the
term *divine drama.* As Ezekiel proclaimed: "I the Lord bring low the
high tree, and make high the low tree, dry up the green tree, and make
the dry tree flourish" (Ezek. 17:24).

The biblical heroes, who loom very large to the child in Sunday
school, are really not heroes in the grand sense of the tragic hero or
noble hero or mythological hero. They are, at best, on the order of the
large frog in a small pond. Biblical heroes are often ordinary, if not
insignificant and unlikely, people who are used as common vessels for
the work of God. They more closely resemble clay pots than golden
goblets. The forebears of Israel—Abraham, Isaac, and Jacob—were
nomadic shepherds which, if not exactly at the bottom of the social order, were certainly on the outer circumference. Nomadic shepherds
grazed their herds on the less desirable, less arable land at the edges of
the desert, the rugged hills, or the roadways.

In the story of Abraham and Lot, Abraham chose the less fertile
land of Canaan rather than the lush Jordan River valley, adjacent to
Sodom and Gomorrah. Canaan, even where dotted with small villages

and cities, was hardly a center of high culture. The metropolises of civilized advancement lay elsewhere: Egypt, Sumeria, Assyria, Babylonia, Persia, Greece, and Rome. Canaan was more of a corridor framed by the Mediterranean and the desert over which caravans and armies traveled between the empires of the day. During the first millennium B.C. and on into the first millennium A.D., Israel was much like a Third World country under the domination of a succession of superpowers, each larger and more powerful than the preceding. Only in the time of Solomon in the tenth century B.C. had Israel briefly approached significant stature in the Middle East. That grand display of imperial glory proved in many ways to be a mixed blessing.

Most of the people who marched in the biblical parade were nobodies and the prophets of nobodies. They were not the builders of the great pyramids and treasure houses of Egypt, except insofar as they may have worked on them as slaves. Some were later to live in the shadow of the magnificent palaces and pyramid-temples of Mesopotamia as exiles in Babylon. They did not enrich the world with the poetry and drama and philosophy that we associate with Greek culture. Nor were they noted for the kinds of engineering feats and road-building projects and organizational skills of the Romans. In the fine arts they were not particularly distinguished in sculpture, painting, music, or craftmanship when compared with any of the great empires of the day. Although the Roman Empire eventually stretched between the British Isles in the west to India in the east, Israel in the Golden Age of King David was roughly the size of Yellowstone National Park. The chosen of God were clearly not chosen because they had the most to offer but because they had little to offer but themselves.

If there were a Chosen People of God Contest today, we might imagine the great nations and former empires coming forth, one by one, each claiming the distinction on the grounds of its many contributions to world civilization. England, France, Germany, Japan, and of course the United States would be among the leading contenders. Russia might not enter on the grounds of official atheism, and Italy might be disqualified for already having been chosen as the seat of the papacy. (Such offers are usually not open to employees and their families.) For Americans the choice would be unmistakably clear, as a century ago it would have been clear to the citizens of the British Empire. The United States would lay claim to the prize as the richest and most powerful nation on earth, champion of democracy, defender of the free world, bastion of capitalism, advocate of human rights, founder of the United Nations, leader in space exploration, and home of the World Series. Could anything be further beyond a reasonable doubt?

The announcement ceremony is scheduled to take place at the United Nations General Assembly. So certain is it that the United States will be the winner, not even counting a president who has advocated school prayer, that the entire executive and legislative branches of government have come to the ceremony. But when the winner of the Chosen People of God Contest is finally announced, it is said to be the people of Namibia!

This scenario is essentially what Paul presents in writing to the young church at Corinth. He takes special note in his introductory remarks that not many members of the church are educated, influential, or highborn. In fact, on the face of it, his remarks sound quite insulting. He does not begin in a flattering manner, observing (whether true or not) that they are an intelligent, impressive-looking congregation, clearly the cream of the crop and the finest examples of the citizenry of Corinth. No, Paul introduces his advice in a way that is contrary to all the rules of *How to Win Friends and Influence People*. He even uses words such as foolish, weak, low and despised, nothing!

> Consider your call, brethren; not many of you were wise according to worldly standards, not many were powerful, not many were of noble birth; but God chose what is foolish in the world to shame the wise, God chose what is weak in the world to shame the strong, God chose what is low and despised in the world, even things that are not, to bring to nothing things that are, so that no human being might boast in the presence of God. (1 Cor. 1:26–29)

This statement summarizes the plot of many a biblical story. On the surface the Apostle's observations might seem open to the charge of anti-Semitism, but in this case they are being made by a Jew who is writing to Gentile as well as Jewish converts. This is the way God often works in the world—in Israel, yes, but also among the Greeks and the Romans. In the humor of God the nations will be blessed not only through Abraham the vagabond and Isaac the ''joke.'' Now, even among Gentiles, an invitation has gone out to the foolish, the weak, the lowly and despised, the nothings of this world, who are called to be God's fools. What a strange choosing and calling!

The Underdog

Many biblical stories suggest this kind of divine comedy. The Word of God is not delivered to the mighty pharaoh of Egypt but to Moses, son of slaves, who has fled prosecution as a murderer and is sheepherding on "the backside of the desert." That Word, furthermore, comes to one who is a stammerer, who is not interested in the job offer, and who because of his speech problem has to speak through his brother Aaron. Yet that Word leads to the defeat of the pharaoh, the death of the firstborn of Egypt, and the emancipation of the Hebrew slaves. How the mighty are fallen and the powerless lifted up! It is a message that ever since has given hope to the hopeless and courage to the meek.

In the story of Gideon, a force of 32,000 men is marshaled to repel a Midianite threat, but God insists that the force be reduced, "lest Israel vaunt themselves against me, saying, 'My own hand has delivered me'" (Judg. 7:2). So Gideon reduces the force to 10,000 men. Still that is said to be too many, despite the fact that the Midianites are said to be "like locusts for multitude" and their camels "as the sand which is upon the seashore" (7:12). So a test is devised, which nearly all the soldiers fail, leaving Gideon with but 300 men to fight the Midianite horde. Yet with this small band he surrounds the Midianite encampment during the night and at an appointed signal they hold torches aloft and begin shouting lustily. The sleeping Midianites are thrown into confusion and in the darkness begin to kill one another or to flee, giving the victory to Gideon's "mission impossible."

Later, when the people clamor for a king in order to be "like all the nations," the reluctant prophet Samuel anoints the young Saul, whose principal distinction seems to be that he is tall and handsome. Saul's response, however, is to point out that he is "from the least of the tribes of Israel" and his family "the humblest of all the families of the tribe of Benjamin" (1 Sam. 9:21). Furthermore, when all the tribes are assembled for the selection of the king, Saul is so reluctant that he hides himself among the baggage.

The quintessential example, of course, is that of David and Goliath. Saul may have been tall, but the Philistine Goliath was a giant, described as nearly ten feet tall, with a bronze coat of mail weighing 150 pounds and a spear the size of a pole. When the braggart Goliath challenged the Israelite army, not one soldier dared to accept the challenge. All shrank back in fear. David, only a shepherd boy and the youngest son of Jesse, learned of the humiliation of the Israelite army as he delivered lunches to his older brothers on the field of battle. Young David said he was not afraid of the giant and persuaded King Saul to allow him to accept the challenge. Goliath scoffed at a mere boy approaching him without armor, without training, and without experience. "Am I a dog, that you come to me with sticks?" Boastingly, he called out to David, "I will give your flesh to the birds of the air and to the beasts of the field" (1 Sam. 17:43, 44). As the proud Philistine strode toward him, David placed a small stone in his slingshot and with a single throw felled the giant with a blow to the forehead.

Comedy is the great leveler. Giants are felled, and underlings are victorious. Tyrants are defeated and slaves liberated. Beautiful people are splattered with mud and Cinderellas fitted with glass slippers. Despite our love of greatness, the Bible does not offer the kind of heroic literature that emphasizes and eulogizes human greatness. The Bible, in fact, has very little good to say about human greatness. Given instead are warnings about putting too much faith and trust in human strength, wisdom, and achievement. Evil is the most likely, indeed inevitable, result of pride, arrogance, and boastfulness. "Pride goes before destruction, and a haughty spirit before a fall" (Prov. 16:18). Like comedy, the biblical impulse is to find foolishness in wisdom and wisdom in foolishness. Ballooning egos are deflated, despots dethroned, the pompous are tripped up, and those in authority are left powerless and whimpering. "When pride comes, then comes disgrace; but with the humble is wisdom" (Prov. 11:2).

The word *humble*, unfortunately, has tended to lose its full meaning, particularly in a culture that idolizes number-oneness. A humble person conjures up images of one who is timid, shy, withdrawn, self-effacing; someone who is easily dominated, a pushover. It seems reasonable to assume that if the proud are those who think highly of themselves, the humble must be those who think lowly of themselves. To be humble is to sit under a private dark cloud, muttering, "I'm nobody, nothing, and less than nothing." Did not Jesus respond to being addressed as "Good Teacher" by saying "Why do you call me good? No one is good but God alone" (Mark 10:18)? Did not Paul, relentless founder of churches and writer of epistles, say "I am the foremost of sinners" (1 Tim. 1:15)?

The difficulty with such a view is that self-effacement alone is like exchanging masochism for sadism. The choices are either to beat up on someone else or to beat up on oneself! To identify a person as humble is not to detract from that person's dignity and worth—that would be humiliation, as in the quip (attributed to Churchill) about Chamberlain and his policies of appeasement to Adolf Hitler: "He is a humble man, with much to be humble about." To speak of the humble is to speak of a dignity and worth that those who are proud would take away. A proud person is one who says, "Relative to me, you have little value and importance; relative to my genius and achievement, you are nothing." Thus Jesus says that the proud will be humbled but the humble will be exalted. That is, their true dignity and worth will be appreciated and vindicated. They will no longer be deprecated by the proud.

Humility is not thinking lowly of oneself; it is not thinking of oneself. Humility takes congratulations in stride and changes the subject. After all, thinking highly of oneself and thinking lowly of oneself have one thing in common—"I" is the center of attention. The humble person is not one who grovels in the dust and wears moth-eaten jackets but one who has ceased being concerned about the question of being superior or inferior to someone else. The humble person is free, free to be concerned about others, free to be at the disposal of others, free to see the worth in others.

When the disciples were on their way to eat the Passover with Jesus in the Upper Room on the eve of his crucifixion, they were busily quarreling among themselves over which one would "sit at the right hand" of Jesus when he entered his kingdom. They were imagining positions of great power and influence just around the corner. So busy were they with the question of their own importance and future glory that they had not prepared for the small details of the Passover, such as who would wash the feet of those who entered the room. Washing the feet of guests was traditionally a servant's job; but the disciples were on their way to becoming rulers, not foot washers. Jesus, having seen that no provision had been made and that no disciple had offered, took the pitcher, towel, and basin and began to wash his disciples' feet. Jesus readily assumed the position of a servant because he was not thinking only of himself—though in those dark circumstances he had every right to be preoccupied with his own coming ordeal.

A story is told of the esteemed Japanese Christian leader, Takeoka Kagawa, arising out of an American speaking tour. Dr. Kagawa had written many books, had been a notable church leader, and had received international recognition as a Christian spokesperson. On one occasion he had been scheduled to address a large convention of clergy and lay leaders. Before the service he and the denominational officials who were to escort him to the platform stopped in the restroom. As often happens at a large convention, many of the men who had been in the restroom that day had missed the trashcan with their paper towels. When Dr. Kagawa's escorts left the restroom for the platform, they assumed he was right behind them. When they reached the platform, however, he was nowhere in sight. Returning to the restroom, they found Dr. Kagawa carefully picking up all the papers that others had left for the janitor!

Neither Jesus' washing his disciples' feet nor Dr. Kagawa's picking up trash was a heroic deed. Both were simple, menial acts. Both men had pressing matters on their minds. They could easily have been excused if they had ignored such seemingly trivial details. Yet they were not so concerned about themselves or their self-images that they had no time for small acts of thoughtfulness. To such a spirit, small deeds are as important as large deeds. The washing of dusty feet is placed on the same level as the lifting of the bread and the cup. Paper towels weigh as much as sermons and speeches.

Collapsing the Categories

We live in a world that often moves in the opposite direction from the world of the Bible. We are enamored of superheroes and reaching the top of the competitive pile. All people and achievements are sorted out on scales of value, whether graded from one to ten or divided by a simplistic use of antonyms—important and unimportant, beautiful and ugly, winners and losers, rich and poor, somebodies and nobodies. We construct educational systems that aim not so much to reward students for working to their full potential—whatever that might be—but to rank students according to their ability and achievement: superior to inferior, A to F. We develop athletic programs whose goal is not getting participants to play to the limits of their individual skills but classifying athletes relative to one another, with the ultimate goal of defeating opponents as a demonstration of superiority. Similarly we measure personal worth and success by the size of bank accounts and houses, rungs on the corporate ladder, career achievements. We carry about with us a variety of mental yardsticks with which we are constantly measuring everyone and everything.

Jesus had little interest in the usual worldly wisdom in these matters or patience with those whose consuming passion was the question of where they stood on some human pyramid. On another occasion when he heard his disciples quarreling among themselves over who would be the greatest in the coming kingdom, Jesus led a small child into their midst and interrupted their discussion by saying, "he who is least among you all is the one who is great" (Luke 9:48). This is the same comic reversal as in the episode in which women brought their children to Jesus "that he might touch them." Jesus' disciples were certain that Jesus had more important things to do than to pay attention to small children. When the disciples attempted to send them away Jesus said indignantly, "Let the children come to me, do not hinder them; for to such belongs the kingdom of God" (Mark 10:14).

Comic reversals are to be found throughout Jesus' relationships. In the story about Zaccheus, the most despised man in the village was invited to have tea with Jesus, when all others in the village would have seen themselves as more worthy objects of Jesus' attentions. Jesus, in the parable of the Good Samaritan, chose as a hero the least likely candidate, since a "good Jew" in Jesus' time would have no dealings with a Samaritan. Yet it was the despised Samaritan who helped the distressed man lying by the roadside. The "good Jews"—the priest and the Levite—walked by on the other side.

In another incident Jesus asked water of a Samaritan woman of doubtful repute on his journey through Samaria, although an orthodox Jew would not have set foot in Samaria or touched water poured by a Samaritan, let alone offered by a woman who had had five husbands and was living with a man not her husband. Understandably the woman was surprised and asked, "How is it that you, a Jew, ask a drink of me, a woman of Samaria?" (John 4:9). In fact, Jesus' relationship to publicans, sinners, and adulterers was quite unorthodox, even topsy-turvy. When the Pharisees brought a woman "caught in adultery" to test Jesus' attitude toward Mosaic law (which commanded that such a person be stoned), Jesus at first refused to respond at all but "wrote with his finger on the ground." When pressed for a response, he offered the ultimate rejoinder: "Let him who is without sin among you be the first to throw a stone at her." After her accusers had left, Jesus asked, "Has no one condemned you?" The woman said, "No one, Lord." Then Jesus said, "Neither do I condemn you" (John 8:7–11).

Another familiar collapsing of categories is contained in Jesus' parable of the Pharisee and the publican who came to the temple to pray. The righteous Pharisee, standing proudly, thanked God that he was not like other men—"extortioners, unjust, adulterers, or even like this tax collector"—but instead was one who fasted twice a week and gave tithes of all he possessed. The publican did not even lift up his eyes but cried out, "God, be merciful to me a sinner!" (Luke 18:11–13). To Jesus it is the sinner who is justified, not the righteous.

Jesus dealt in a similar manner with other categories, such as significant and insignificant. Jesus once stood with his disciples, observing those coming to the temple. Some worshipers, no doubt, came with large amounts of gold and silver to place in the offering chest at the entrance to the temple. Jesus did not comment on these, however; instead, he noticed a woman whom no one else had noticed. She was a widow, which, in those days, usually implied poverty. She was probably embarrassed because she had only two half-pennies to contribute. She had likely waited to one side until those who were able to give generously had passed, hoping that no one would notice her. But someone did notice her, not to look down upon her and the trivial sum she had to bring, but to call attention to her generosity. Jesus noticed her, and he said to his disciples, "This poor widow has put in more than all those who are contributing to the treasury. For they all contributed out of their abundance; but she out of her poverty has put in everything she had, her whole living" (Mark 12:43, 44).

By the comparative standards of the secular world, Jesus' evaluation is nonsense. How can two half-pennies be said to outweigh the thousands of shekels of gold and silver that had been poured into the treasury that day? This is not the way things are done at the First National Bank. Such a method of calculation would guarantee a stock market crash. Yet there is a higher scale of values, and on this divine scale, it is so.

The story of the widow is like the story of the church that was having a fund-drive to build a new sanctuary. The giving and pledging had not been coming in as needed, and too many people were saying, "Let someone else pay for it—someone who has more money." The minister aired the problem from the pulpit and made an impassioned plea for greater generosity. The next Sunday one of the ushers handed the minister a note from a boy of seven who had heard the minister's exhortation on giving. A coin was taped to the note, which read: "I'm glad you are making a new church. I want to help, too. Here is a nickel. Your friend, Johnny." At the bottom of the note he had added a P.S.: "If you need any more, let me know." The minister was not only amused but touched by the note, and when he read it in church the following Sunday, the congregation was so moved that they shortly raised enough additional pledges and gifts to pay for the new sanctuary.

On the divine scale a boy's nickel may be worth more than thousand-dollar donations. A poor widow's pennies may outweigh talents of gold and silver. Children may be closer to the kingdom of heaven than Jesus' own disciples. Tea is taken with publicans rather than people of high repute. Sinners are justified instead of the righteous. Adulterers and prostitutes are forgiven; their accusers are sent abruptly away. Untouchable Samaritans are touched or become moral examples. Fools are wiser than the wise, and the weak stronger than the strong. Nobodies stand up and are counted; somebodies are set aside and ignored. And the meek inherit the earth.

If one were to summarize this divine comedy in a single story, it might go something like this. God announced that a people were to be chosen through whom the divine will was to be revealed and the divine work to be done. Then God called all the peoples of the earth to present their credentials. The great nations responded by sending special envoys to display their wares and to tell of their glorious achievements. The envoys lauded the genius of their political and social systems, the superiority of their scientific and technological advancements, the vast reaches of their empires and their military exploits, the marvels of their pyramids and palaces, the beauty of their sculpture and art, the grandeur of their holy temples. Egypt, Assyria, Babylon, Persia, Greece, Rome—all were represented.

God said to the assembled envoys, "I have determined to choose a people from your midst. I will come and visit my people, and will dwell among them, and will be their God. Through them I will work great works and reveal great things." The representatives of each nation went back to their people with the good news, each feeling assured of being chosen. In every great nation the people swelled with pride. They made large offerings in their temples and prepared lavish celebrations. Gold and silver were brought into the sacred treasuries, musicians were rehearsed, and an abundance of sheep and oxen were sacrificed. The air was filled with the smell of fat beasts and the noise of songs and instruments. "Surely," they said to one another, "we are the people and servants of God."

The people of all the great nations prepared a grand welcome and a lavish celebration. They assembled all their most important and impressive people. Their kings and queens were seated in royal splendor, surrounded by the magnificence of the court and nobility. In procession before them came the high priests and magicians in full regalia, the advisers and astrologers and officials of state, the judges and administrators of provinces, the architects of their great buildings and taskmasters of their public projects, the generals and admirals of their armed forces, along with the wealthiest of their merchants and landowners. They paraded their military heroes, their legions of marching soldiers, and all their finest instruments of war. They paraded, too, the captives of their recent conquests—men, women, and children in chains—slaves for the market and the quarries and for the amusement of the crowd.

God entered the capitals of each of these great nations in turn. And God walked right past the royal highnesses and the noble lords and the reverend priests. God walked right past the dignitaries and officers and cheering crowds, past the platforms, the processions, and the instruments of war. Suddenly the gala parade was brought to a confused standstill, and the cheering of the crowd became a puzzled murmur. As a profound hush fell over the vast assembly, God began to release the chains of the prisoners, one by one—children, men and women, young and old. And God said, "These are my people. These are the people of God."

Then, turning aside, God led them into the side streets and back alleys. The motley parade was joined by the poor and the sick and the lame, by slaves and beggars and women of the night, and by little children playing in the streets. It was joined by all those not invited or counted or included. And God said to them, "You are the chosen of God, for you have nothing to offer me but yourselves."

4

Mary
Had
a
Little
Lamb

Less than a century and a half ago Christmas was not celebrated in many Protestant churches. Not only were the secular additions to Christmas frowned upon, there were no religious observances. In fact, the two most controversial issues being debated in some of our churches prior to the Civil War were slavery and the celebration of Christmas. Presumably the more liberal ministers of the time were for Christmas and against slavery; the more conservative ministers were against Christmas and for slavery!

The main arguments against observing Christmas were that most of the customs were of pagan origin; that too much drinking and merry-making were associated with the season; and that the Catholics, Episcopalians, and Lutherans did it. Earlier in American history the Puritans, while inspiring the observation of Thanksgiving, had even passed a law against making merry during the Yuletide season. The year was 1659.

> Whosoever shall be found observing any such day as Christmas and the like, either by feasting, forbearing labor, or any other way . . . every such person so offending shall pay for each offense five shillings as a fine to the country.

Insofar as these objections were grounded in concern that the meaning of Christ's birth not get buried under an avalanche of customs and celebrations, the concern has certainly proved to be prophetic. The problem is not just the pagan customs or the secular additions, however. It is also the crushing weight of endless religious songs, stories, and entertainments that overwhelm the simplicity and humbleness of a birth that, at the time, went largely unnoticed.

The event of the birth of Christ has been so elevated by pious imagination and surrounded by angelic hosts, beatific halos, and paeans of praise that the utter lowliness and obscurity of the circumstances are difficult to conceive. The meager nativity scene has become so crowded with shepherds, Wise Men, angels, animals, gifts, children's pageants, and gaily decorated trees that we cannot feel how lonely that night was. From Bethlehem itself proceeds such a bedlam of mooing cows, braying donkeys, baaing sheep, calling birds, Ave Marias, and angelic alleluias that the silence of that silent night cannot be heard.

Yet a part of the foolishness of God, a part of the divine folly that we preach, is there nevertheless. We do not easily notice the foolishness, for the story is so familiar, so comfortably blanketed in all the sentiments of Christmas, so festooned with all the pagan, secular, and sacred additions to the season. This birth has become such a normal, annually rehearsed event in the liturgical year, not to mention the shopping year, that it no longer surprises us or speaks to us. We forget what an improbable, almost preposterous, story it is.

We reaffirm, as a matter of course and with all the smoothness of trained ministerial intonation, the incredible tale. In some mysterious way, in an infant born to a poor peasant girl in a donkey shed in a small, remote town in a minor province among a conquered people of no particular importance, God was specially present. Emmanuel, God with us. What divine foolishness is this?

Is it any wonder that this message has been "a stumbling block to Jews and folly to Gentiles" (1 Cor. 1:23)? Is *this* where anyone would have thought to look? Could the wisdom of the Greek philosophers or the messianic expectations of the Jews have traced such esoteric clues and meandering migrations as to pinpoint this obscure spot on the globe and this unlikely cast of characters? It is as if this were an instance of a divine hide-and-seek rather than self-manifestation, of God hidden rather than God revealed.

The Wisdom of the Magi

The natural human inclination in looking for God—if God is looked for at all—is to look in the circumstances of special power and importance. We immediately think in terms of places that seem suggestive of the glory of God or places that might be worthy of the divine presence. We imagine people of status and stature, with whom we, and perhaps even God, might be impressed. Yet in the nativity stories of Matthew and Luke we are given neither. We are given, if anything, the opposite. We are shown some very *unlikely* people and places. Instead of a royal entourage and red-carpet treatment, we are shown peasants and straw beds and the back door. Such is the comic surprise.

When the Wise Men in their wisdom came, having seen a bright star in the western sky, which they took as a sign of a royal birth, where was it that they looked first? In the palace of King Herod, of course. Where the Wise Men looked is where all of us tend to look. Yet in the Bible the places where God appeared again and again were where people were *not* looking: in lowly places, out-of-the-way places, forgotten places, despised places, godforsaken places.

God appeared to Abraham, Isaac, and Jacob—illiterate shepherds on the desert fringes of the great civilizations of the ancient world. God appeared among slaves in the slums and the labor camps of Egypt. God appeared in the midst of a captive Jewry in exile in Babylon. God appeared among a subject people in Roman-occupied Palestine, far removed from the luxury of Herod's palace, let alone the grandeur of Caesar's Rome. One thing can be said for certain about the God of the Bible: this is a God who rarely travels first-class!

We expect a royal birth, a messianic figure, the Son of God. We expect one of whom it can clearly be said that "his name will be called Wonderful Counselor, Mighty God, Everlasting Father, Prince of Peace" (Isa. 9:6). We are shown instead a child born at the bottom of the social and political orders of the time, living amid a subject people in a distant and inconsequential outpost of the vast Roman Empire. Even here we are not taken to the mansion of the provincial governor or the palace of the tributary Jewish king. We are shown a carpenter's young wife, come from a poor village, the humble status of which—even among Jews—is suggested by the phrase later thrown at Jesus: "Can anything good come out of Nazareth?" (John 1:46). Understandably, Mary had exclaimed: "[God] has regarded the low estate of his handmaiden" (Luke 1:48).

Far from silken palaces and royal pleasure groves, this child is not even born in his own home, humble as that was, but in Bethlehem after Mary and Joseph have made an arduous journey to register for the Roman census. There is no coterie of servants, physicians, midwives, and maids-in-waiting. There is no one to help but Joseph—what little help he is—and no place for them but a back alley. Where is this child to be found, but among the lowliest of the low? Indeed he is found among animals, in a bed of straw, midst the scent of manure.

How strangely out of place are the Wise Men's gifts for this child: gold, frankincense, and myrrh! These are gifts for the child who has everything, who is cradled in fine cloth and who will be fed with a silver spoon. These are the gifts of the rich to the rich. Well-intended as they are and appropriate to Jesus' royal lineage, they are like giving gold medals and expensive perfumes and lace evening dresses to the starving and homeless of Africa.

This is how God came and how God comes: in the lowly and lonely places, the dark hours, among little things. Here is that weakness of God that is stronger than the strength of humans and that foolishness of God that destroys the wisdom of the wise and brings to nothing the understanding of the prudent. The words of Mary's prayer at the annunciation are characteristic, not only of the nature of the nativity but of many biblical stories:

> "He has scattered the proud in the imagination of their hearts,
> he has put down the mighty from their thrones,
> and exalted those of low degree;
> he has filled the hungry with good things,
> and the rich he has sent empty away."
>
> (Luke 1:51–53)

Even though Jesus' lineage is traced to the royal line of David, why is it that the Gospels go to such great pains to emphasize the meager circumstances of his parentage and birth? We might expect some attempt at glorification of certain biographical details and a minimizing of others. The story might have been presented solely in the grand terms of John's Gospel, diverting attention from the obscurity of his birth altogether: "And the Word became flesh and dwelt among us, full of grace and truth; we have beheld his glory, glory as of the only Son from the Father" (John 1:14).

At the very least, the more humble and humiliating aspects of Jesus' birthplace, family, and home village might have been glossed over. It could have been intimated that Jesus had come from one of the "better families" of Nazareth and one of the "more desirable locations in town." Perhaps the "fine craftmanship and cabinetry" of his father could have been lauded and phrases such as "highly respected" and "outstanding citizens of the community" could have been used of the families of Joseph and Mary. Was there not also a posh Roman bath nearby in Galilee that they could have been associated with?

There are always those who come forth to try to make the picture more rose-colored than it is. A recent book advertised in the *London Times Magazine* proposes to prove that (1) "the Jesus Family were wealthy people"; (2) "the disciples were rich and/or influential . . . none were simple fishermen"; (3) "Mary was not a simple innocent, unaware small town Jewish girl—she was in fact used to rubbing shoulders with the wealthy, attending parties, singing, dancing and drinking wine"; (4) "a member of the British Royal Family was the first Bishop of Rome"; and (5) "Jesus was of English descent—his grandmother was born in Cornwall . . . and the grave of the Virgin Mary's uncle was found at Glastonbury." The *London Times* advertisement is accommodating enough to note also that the author "is better known as a successful businessman, a millionaire, an entrepreneur and a prolific writer of books on business psychology—all [of which] have been outstanding successes."[1]

Yes, according to the Gospels, Jesus was of royal descent—though nothing is mentioned of English descent, the British Royal Family, Cornwall, or Glastonbury. Nor did any notice of his birth appear in the society section of the *London Times*. Nor for that matter were his disciples listed in the *Palestinian Social Register* or the *Who's Who in the Roman Empire*. They were fishermen, carpenters, tax collectors, revolutionary zealots, unskilled laborers, without school diplomas or investment portfolios. Jesus characterizes the affluence of his ministry among them by saying, "Foxes have holes, and birds of the air have nests; but the Son of man has nowhere to lay his head" (Luke 9:58). Jesus also paid his taxes by taking a coin from a fish's mouth. It is unlikely that Jesus made many trips to England on this kind of budget.

Even the genealogies Matthew and Luke used to give Jesus a royal lineage are a "mixed bag." Nothing is known about a third of the names one way or another, but another third are names well known as evil kings in the house of Judah. If we take Matthew's list, David's son Solomon is already a very ambiguous figure, obsessed with opulence and bringing considerable idolatry into Israel through his large harem of pagan wives. Solomon's son Rehoboam was a harsh taskmaster over his people and is described in 2 Chronicles as one who "forsook the law of the LORD" (12:1) and who "did evil, for he did not set his heart to seek the LORD" (12:14). His grandson Asa is said to have "inflicted cruelties upon some of the people" (16:10). The rule of Asa's grandson Jehoram is summarized by saying, "he did what was evil in the sight of the LORD" (21:6) and "departed with no one's regret" (21:20). And of Jehoram's great-grandson Ahaz it is said, "he did not do what was right in the eyes of the LORD" (28:1). Jesus had quite an array of skeletons in his genealogical closet!

It would be no surprise, furthermore, if—in addition to attempting to suppress details that might be damaging to Jesus' image—the stories of his birth had been embellished, after the fashion of heroic myth, with all manner of marvels and miracles. A trace of such embellishment is there, but in a remarkably subdued and almost matter-of-fact form: a birth announcement, a brilliant star, an angelic chorus. Jesus is not presented as coming on the scene of Roman occupation in the might and majesty of the superhero, with the sound of trumpets and a blaze of glory. Not surprisingly there were those who asked among themselves, What kind of a Messiah is this? The Jesus of the Gospels did not look at all like a heroic deliverer or an anointed king but, if anything, more like a suffering servant to whom the words of Isaiah 53 might well be applied:

> For he grew up before him like a young plant,
>   and like a root out of dry ground;
> he had no form or comeliness that we should look at him,

and no beauty that we should desire him.
He was despised and rejected by men;
    a man of sorrows, and acquainted with grief;
and as one from whom men hide their faces
    he was despised, and we esteemed him not.
                                        (Isa. 53:2–3)

In the works of great literature, these are hardly the epithets applied to
the mighty heroes of epic or the noble heroes of drama or the fabulous
heroes of mythological lore. These are the descriptions of victims, not
victors. These are the titles most aptly given to the poor and the meek
and the persecuted.

The Bottom of the Pile

The realities presented in Matthew and Luke are that scarcely anyone noticed the birth. The last word from the innkeeper in Bethlehem
was that there was no room. Those crowded into the inn that night were
either merrymaking or asleep and in any event were oblivious to the
condition of a young woman great with child. No eager multitude
clamored outside for the first news. There was no welcome by the town
fathers. Not a single priest or scribe, Pharisee or Sadducee, was aware
of the moment. Certainly the event made not the slightest ripple in the
house of the Roman governor, let alone the palace of Caesar. The birth
was noticed only by a few simple shepherds from the nearby hills and
some distant astrologers who arrived a year later and knocked on the
wrong door.

Jesus' nativity was *brought* to the attention of King Herod as a result of the mistaken inquiry by the Magi, but instead of Herod's promised homage, Mary and Joseph were forced to flee with the child Jesus
into Egypt to escape the threatened slaughter of young male children.
The angelic alleluia echoed rather coldly and feebly in that landscape:

"Glory to God in the highest,
and on earth peace among men with
    whom he is pleased!"
                                        (Luke 2:14)

Jesus' childhood and young manhood were similarly undistin-
guished and unnoticed. Only two other people are mentioned as having

acknowledged Jesus' birth, on the occasion of his circumcision eight days later at the temple. One was an elderly prophetess, Anna, who lived by the temple, the other an elderly man, Simeon (Luke 2:25–38), neither of them people of any consequence. Beyond this, and except for a brief mention that Jesus at age twelve astonished the teachers in the temple with his mature answers (Luke 2:41–51), nobody seemed to have taken any special notice of him until his ministry. In his youth Jesus worked as an apprentice in his father's carpenter shop, probably making plain and simple furniture. Perhaps later, as a young man, he continued to work as a carpenter to care for his widowed mother and her younger children. We do not know much of Jesus' early life, and presumably no one of his day did either.

Piety rushes in to fill these blank spaces with tales of wonder that might rescue the image of Jesus from humble origins and an ordinary life—as did later apocryphal stories that attributed marvels to him, such as making clay birds fly (Gospel of Thomas). Yet the relative lowliness and uneventfulness of his early life remain. For thirty years Jesus lived in oblivion as a typical lower-class Jewish youth in the inconsequential village of Nazareth, making boxes and stools. The blank spaces, the lack of notice, the obscurity, the insignificance, are in themselves significant.

Why such simplicity of story and humbleness of circumstance? If the effect is any clue, the reason is this: it is possible for anyone, no matter how poor or powerless or oppressed, to identify with this child. No one could feel awkward and uncomfortable in his presence. No one could stand outside this life, this story. Jesus is not presented as barely getting his feet wet in the human condition—as we sometimes do when the water is cold and we put our toes in and say we have been swimming. Jesus is presented in the Gospels as being immersed in the total human condition. He has dived into the depths of human life.

Who, then, could be lonely, and Jesus had not been lonely? Who could be ignored, and Jesus had not been ignored? Who could be poor, and he had not been poor? Who could be oppressed, and he had not been oppressed? Who could have nowhere to lay his head, and Jesus, too, had had nowhere to lay his head? Who could be despised and rejected, and he had not been despised and rejected? Who could be persecuted, and he had not been persecuted? Who could suffer and he had not suffered? Who could be betrayed and mocked and killed, and he had not been betrayed and mocked and killed? Who could be forsaken, and Jesus had not also cried out, "My God, my God, why hast thou forsaken me?"

One is reminded of the approach to the masses taken by the great Indian leader Mahatma Gandhi. Gandhi acknowledged that he had been much influenced by the Gospels and touched by the life of Christ. As he once remarked, "I might have become a Christian had it not been for the Christians!" Ironically, one of the clearest examples of a Christ-like life to which one can point in the twentieth century is this Hindu mahatma ("great soul"). Even when Gandhi became one of the principal leaders of India and an internationally renowned figure, he continued to dress in the simplest peasant clothing and had few possessions beyond his spectacles, writing instruments, and some books. Much of the time he walked—as the poor walked—rather than ride in vehicles or trains. When he did ride he often insisted on the crowded third-class passage, which in the India of the time was almost like riding in a cattle car.

Gandhi did not lead the masses by standing imperiously and luxuriously above them but by identifying with them and sharing in their circumstances. A part of Gandhi's greatness was that not even the untouchables of India were beneath him or were made to feel uneasy in his presence. Other Indian leaders lived in mansions, far removed from the masses, going everywhere and doing everything first-class, but Gandhi would not allow anyone to be lower than he. Other Indian dignitaries, usually of high caste themselves, were no more willing to associate with untouchables than with lepers, but Gandhi not only lived and marched with untouchables but gave them a new dignity and a new name. He called them *harijans*, "the people of God." This was Gandhi's foolishness, a foolishness for which he was often criticized by the wise and noble and powerful of India.

The God of the Bible is like that. God moved through the pages of biblical history in third class. God did not ride in the palanquins of pharaohs or the processions of kings or the chariots of conquering heroes. God walked with the slave peoples of Egypt and the captive peoples of Babylon and the conquered peoples of Rome. And these people were called a chosen people, "the people of God." This is God's foolishness, the foolishness of God that is wiser than human wisdom and the weakness of God that is stronger than human strength.

The Prince and the Pauper

There is another dimension, however. Jesus is not exclusively identified with the lowly. The noble and powerful and wise are not entirely left out. They may be included on the same basis as everyone else, if they are willing to stand with everyone else. The Bible is quite equalitarian on this point. Jesus is, after all, said to be of the house and lineage of David. He is therefore in some deeply hidden way a prince to whom all the epithets of royal birth and regal promise can be applied:

> For to us a child is born,
>   to us a son is given;
> and the government will be upon his shoulder. . . .
> (Isa. 9:6)

Jesus is presented in the Gospels as one who is not simply and totally defined by the status of the poor and oppressed. He is presented, rather, as one who incarnates the whole of the human spectrum. Whether a person is at the top or the bottom of the social order, no one can stand outside this life. Whether powerful or powerless, important or unimportant, great or small, all are embraced in this single figure. Jesus is said to be of royal birth, with nowhere to lay his head. He is of the house and lineage of David, born in an animal shed. Above is a brilliant star and angelic chorus; beneath is straw and dirt and the smell of manure.

The sense of this first came to me, as realizations often do, in a rather mundane setting: a viewing of one of Chaplin's silent films. Strange theological textbook! For many years Chaplin captivated film audiences with the paradoxical figure of the Tramp. The Tramp became one of the most beloved figures in the world, with his clipped moustache and soulful eyes set in a pallid face, his shabby but once elegant clothes, his jaunty penguin gait, his dusty dignity. One day it dawned on me what Charlie's secret was, and it was a very biblical secret. Chaplin had put together in his costuming and behavior the bowler hat, dress coat, and bow tie of English aristocracy, along with the baggy pants, floppy shoes, and disheveled appearance of the gutter bum. Chaplin was not simply a tramp but a gentleman-tramp. The top and the bottom of the social order were completely contained in one person who was both gentleman and tramp, somebody and nobody at the same time. The most extreme ends of the human spectrum were juxtaposed and united in one slender figure. This was the essence of his comedy.

Basically Charlie was the Tramp, sleeping on park benches or in flophouses or police stations. He lived among the poor and homeless, orphans and fugitives, ex-convicts and hoboes, the unemployed and the hungry. This was the world of most of his films from 1914 to 1940, as it had been the world of his childhood in the London slums of Kennington. Yet there was another side that shone through the crumpled figure of the Tramp. There was also the gentleman who wore a tuxedo, albeit threadbare, who could play the part of the man of sophistication and means. Despite the patches and wrinkles he was one who had beauty and grace and manners, who tipped his hat to ladies—but also to babies and cows and fence posts. Even in his most destitute moments he possessed an irrepressible dignity and style.

This is why his films had such universal appeal. Chaplin succeeded in symbolically incarnating the total human condition, top to bottom. He was, as Robert Payne said of him, "the whole human comedy wrapped in a single frail envelope of flesh."[2] No one could stand outside his comedy, and no one was left out. In his dress and comportment Charlie had placed a parenthesis around all levels of human being. All could identify with him because all were included in his person and in his performance.

In a similar way the Gospels stress that Jesus was both king and commoner, of royal blood yet born among peasants, the prince and the pauper. In him all stations were contained and united, all barriers broken down. No one could stand outside the contours of his life, and no one was left outside his reconciliation. Is this not, perhaps, the symbolic significance of the two contrasting groups that visited the Christ Child in Bethlehem, the shepherds and the Wise Men?

Shepherds have been given an unusually exalted place in our imaginations. They boldly and colorfully grace our nativity scenes and Christmas pageants. Jesus, too, is depicted as a shepherd, gently holding a lamb in his arms, like "the LORD is my shepherd" of the psalmist. Yet sheepherding in Jesus' time was among the lowlier occupations. Even more lowly was it in the larger context of the Roman Empire. To be sure, the Jewish heritage is traced to the shepherd forebears—Abraham, Isaac, and Jacob—and much is made of shepherds and sheep in the Bible. Still, the life of the shepherd existed on the perimeter of the civilizations of antiquity. Shepherds lived outside the mainstream of history and the great social and political movements of the high cultures of the day.

The shepherds that came in that night from the hills around Bethlehem would have been about as removed as anyone could be from the larger issues and currents of Roman-occupied Israel. They were hardly men of influence or of stature in the community. They would have had little education and probably could not read or write. Surely they knew nothing of the Roman poets Virgil and Ovid or of the Greek philosophers Plato and Aristotle or the celebrated playwrights Aeschylus and Sophocles. The farthest journey they had ever made was likely little more than the few miles to Jerusalem. They were simple, humble people living simple, humble lives. Yet it was they who were the first to find the Christ Child.

The Wise Men offer a striking contrast to the shepherds. Though they were not the "three kings of Orient" in the Christmas carol, they might well have served and been consulted by kings. As priests (magi) from Mesopotamia or Persia, they would have been highly educated, sophisticated, influential. A significant part of their learning and priestly activity would have centered on astrology. They were wealthy enough to mount a caravan for a two-year journey and to bring expensive presents. As astrologers they took the appearance of a brilliant star to mean that a royal birth of some consequence had taken place in the west, and they came to pay homage. It was certainly reasonable on their part to expect that such a birth would take place in a palace. Though they were wrong about the exact location and had to adjust their sights to much humbler circumstances they, too, found the Christ Child. The lowly setting of this paradoxical birth did not exclude the Wise Men, but it did require a different attitude and understanding. They had to abandon human wisdom for the foolishness of God.

Even more broadly, the nativity stories represent the inclusion of what a fifteenth-century morality play would have called "Everyman." Jesus, of the royal house of David, is born in a manger in David's Bethlehem, visited by simple rough-clad shepherds and rich-robed wise men. In Jesus the oppositions between rich and poor, royalty and peasantry, learned and ignorant, are united and transcended. Those human distinctions to which we give such loyalty and importance, which we spend so much of our lives developing and defining and defending, are blurred and set aside by this birth. A common humanity before God is affirmed and celebrated in the presence of this child. In Christ "there is neither Jew nor Greek, there is neither slave nor free" (Gal. 3:28).

Between Enemy Lines

The theme of the reconciliation of opposites comes through the Christmas story at yet another level: the angelic chorus's "on earth peace among men with whom he is pleased!" (Luke 2:14). How strangely those words reverberate through the valleys of Judah, then and today! "Peace among men" where there was and is no peace. The "good news of a great joy" has fallen among forces in perennial conflict, and largely on deaf ears. "Peace," "good news," and "great joy" come in the midst of battle chariots and Roman legions and battering rams. Into this fray is delivered what? An infant in swaddling clothes, lying in a manger, with a bodyguard of inquisitive shepherds and munching animals. This is how God came and how God comes.

During the last days of the Civil War, Confederate and Union forces were battling fiercely outside Richmond. One evening, however, the Confederate forces ceased fire and began to light bonfires along their front lines. Union sentries called across the battle lines, asking why. The answer was cheerfully given in return. The Confederate troops were celebrating the birth of a child to the wife of General George Pickett. When the news filtered back to General Grant of the Union army, he ordered his troops to join in the celebration. So along both Confederate and Union lines, bonfires sent flames dancing into the night. War-weary men drank toasts and sang songs and told stories. From the trenches came the sound of laughter rather than gunfire and singing rather than the groans of the wounded and dying. On both sides soldiers thought of their own homes and families and wondered if they would be seen again.

A baby had temporarily stopped the war. A small echo of "Peace on earth, good will toward men" was heard in the night. The innocence of a newborn child, the joy of birth, the celebration of life and love, had suddenly brought these fighting men back from the sordid world of adult selfishness and stubbornness and bloodshed. The great differences between them, the animosities and hostilities whose only solution seemed to be war, were softened in the presence of an infant who knew none of this and participated in none of this. For a moment in the darkness of death and destruction, antagonists were reconciled to one another and celebrated together across enemy lines.

This, too, is the foolishness of God, who comes not with military might and heroic deeds but in the weak and helpless form of an infant, born, as it were, on the battlefields of Canaan. How, in fact, should one behave in the presence of a child, even the Christ Child, except by becoming more childlike: a little less hateful and a little more loving, a little less selfish and a little more generous, a little less distrustful and a little more innocent. Then the words of Isaiah might at last be fulfilled: "and a little child shall lead them" (Isa. 11:6).

5

The
Blue
Book
of
Social
Usage

Sometimes in an idle moment I like to browse through old books. The musty smell, the yellowed pages, the quaint turns of phrase, beckon intriguingly from a time that found these words and issues terribly important. One never knows what curiosities may be encountered.

In a browsing mood I once picked up an early edition of Emily Post's *Etiquette: The Blue Book of Social Usage.* I have not been an especially meticulous practitioner of the social graces, nor was I born to high society. Still I was curious about the contents of a book on proper social behavior. Emily Post, after all, was the leading authority on etiquette in the twenties, thirties, and forties. Her words were the bible on the subject.

Expectantly, if not reverently, I opened this hallowed text of worldly wisdom. There I came across this advice on the types of people with whom those in polite society should and should not associate. According to Emily, in giving a party one should aim to make of it "a collection of brilliantly fashionable people." To ensure this she offers a stern word of caution: "The hostess who gathers in all the oddly assorted frumps on the outskirts of society cannot expect to achieve a very distinguished result."[1]

So completely on the outskirts of refined society was I that I had to look up the word *frump*. According to *Funk and Wagnall's Standard Dictionary*—another bible on the subject of polite behavior—a frump is a person who is "dowdily dressed." As a further measure of my distance from refined society, I also had to look up the word *dowdily*. A dowdily dressed person I discovered is one who is "ill-dressed; not neat or fashionable; in bad taste; shabby." Certainly we cannot have such people hanging around or otherwise disturbingly visible! They should be kept out of sight and out of mind, their statistical as well as their real existence denied as far as possible.

The Banquet of God

The Bible and *The Blue Book of Social Usage* apparently belong to different universes. Jesus once offered some advice of his own on the subject. It came out quite differently. This was his counsel on the question of whom one should and should not invite to the party: "When you give a dinner or a banquet, do not invite your friends or your brothers or your kinsmen or rich neighbors." Instead Jesus advised: "when you give a feast, invite the poor, the maimed, the lame, the blind, and you will be blessed, because they cannot repay you" (Luke 14:12–13).

The difference between the wisdom of worldly values and the foolishness of divine values could hardly be stated more clearly. It is nonetheless difficult to find churches that make the distinction so clearly. Whom do we invite to our banquets and potluck suppers except our friends and relatives and rich neighbors? And what is the average church on Sunday morning but "a collection of brilliantly fashionable people"? Is it not, in fact, the church that is commonly cited as one of the social organizations to which the better class of people in the community ought to belong, along with the Masonic Lodge, the Junior League, and the country club?

Jesus said, "it is easier for a camel to go through the eye of a needle than for a rich man to enter the kingdom of God" (Matt. 19:24). In many churches, however, the opposite is more often true. It is easier for a rich man to enter, to assume a position of prominence, and to grace the common worship with all the appointments of our self-indulgence. As Third World theologians have reminded the affluent churches of the West, we have difficulty dealing with the oddly assorted frumps and dowdies that make up much of the human race. They make us feel uncomfortable, uneasy, perhaps queasy. We prefer to be elevated by recountings of human success stories, not the problems of unemployment, poverty, and oppression. Such problems are bad for an upbeat psychology, and also bad for business. If we were to reach out to include those on the outskirts of affluence, how could we maintain our status and self-image in the community? Or if we were actually to give money to the poor rather than invest in our stained-glass windows and air-conditioned sanctuaries and velvet pew cushions and plush carpeting, we could hardly expect to achieve a very distinguished result!

Now and then one hears of an encouraging exception. When the extent of the starvation in drought-stricken Ethiopia became better known in the mid-1980s, a 400-member Baptist church in Belfry, Kentucky, responded. They sent $200,000 to aid the relief work in Ethiopia. The church was not a wealthy church in a wealthy community, without needs of its own, real or imagined. In fact, the church had not even been maintaining a savings account to lay up in store for its own future. Nor had the congregation been in the habit of conducting fund-raising drives for its annual budget or for grand schemes of expansion. Apparently they operated on old-fashioned principles, such as faith and generosity. When an anonymous donor gave $125,000 to the church to spend as it saw fit, instead of using the windfall to refurbish the sanctuary or add building to building, the church deacons voted to send $100,000 of the gift to aid the starving in Ethiopia. Once the benefactor learned of their unselfish benevolence, he donated an additional $100,000 to be sent for famine relief!

Who, by the way, has ever heard of the First Baptist Church of Belfry, Kentucky? Who has heard of Belfry, Kentucky? We have heard of the megachurches across America, with their multimillion-dollar budgets, their architectural wonders, their electronic modernity, their talent for religious extravaganzas. But Belfry, Kentucky?

Worldly Christianity, with its worldly values, is commonplace in church circles, despite considerable braggadocio about upholding traditional values and conserving the moral fiber of the nation. The religious issue, however, is not whether one is "conservative" and "defending the American Way." It is whether one is in fact conserving the morality and values of the biblical tradition. Cadillac ministries, religious entertainment, emotional self-indulgence, lavish church buildings, luxurious appointments, free-enterprise success stories, and American flag-waving are not necessarily identical with the biblical way. An onlooker might at least be permitted to wonder whether modern Christians have been called to become disciples of Christ or of Emily Post.

Too many of our churches are like the modern, progressive church in Peter De Vries' *The Mackeral Plaza*, which contains not only a parlor and gymnasium but a theater, a ballroom, a psychiatric wing, and "a small worship area at one end."[2] Walker Percy offers a similar satire on the American gospel of prosperity, which the most ultrafundamentalist shares with the most secular of humanists. In *Love in the Ruins* both extremes are depicted as having the same material goals, living in the same suburbs, using the same stockbrokers, sharing in many of the same values and aspirations, participating in the same community organizations, and belonging to the same country and tennis clubs.[3] The principal difference, for Percy, between the secular humanist and the secular Christian is that the Christian dresses up on Sunday and goes to church while the humanist puts on old clothes and goes bird watching!

The problem is not unique to the modern American church. In the fourth century Gregory of Nyssa preached against the religiosity of affluence. His text was the third petition of the Lord's Prayer: "Give us this day our daily bread." In the sermon he reminded his hearers that Jesus was not giving an open invitation to include, under a liberal interpretation of "bread," everything we might want. Humorously he chided his congregation:

> So we say to God: Give us bread. Not delicacies or riches, not magnificent purple robes, golden ornaments or precious stones or silver dishes. Nor do we ask him for landed estates, or military commands, or political leadership. We pray neither for herds of horses and oxen or other cattle in great numbers, nor for a host of slaves. We do not say, give us a prominent position in assemblies or monuments and statues raised to us nor silken robes and musicians at our meals . . . [we pray] only [for] bread![4]

Apparently "bread" was already well on its way in the fourth century to becoming slang for money and what money could buy!

Some people have transferred these concerns to the church, as if it were *God* who were interested in such things and we should seek them for God's "house" as well. God, too, is imagined to desire and delight in purple robes and golden ornaments and precious stones and silver dishes, as well as statues, monuments, and musicians. Jesus suggests a somewhat different view of the divine pleasure:

> "Then the King will say to those at his right hand, 'Come, O blessed of my Father, inherit the kingdom prepared for you from the foundation of the world; for I was hungry and you gave me food, I was thirsty and you gave me drink, I was a stranger and you welcomed me, I was naked and you clothed me, I was sick and you visited me, I was in prison and you came to me.' " (Matt. 25:34–36)

No Respecter of Persons

One of the peculiarities of the Bible, among all the religious literature of the world, is that it does not contain a collection of brilliantly fashionable people or the grandiose monuments of human achievement. Instead it contains something more on the order of sheepskin tents, mud-brick villages, and oddly assorted frumps on the outskirts of refined society. In the Bible we are given slaves, refugees, widows, orphans, the lame, the blind, and the halt.

The principal exception is the ambiguous figure of Solomon and the dubiously achieved grandeur of his temple, palace, harem, and stables. The fabulous wealth and accomplishment of Solomon became both the glory and the ignominy of Israel. Jewish pride might swell at the name, and Emily Post might have invited him; yet Solomon's overweening desire for fame and fortune compromised and corrupted Israel. He became a ruler with little to distinguish him from the pharaoh of the Exodus. His celebrated wisdom increasingly turned into a very worldly wisdom: the wisdom of merchants, taskmasters, rulers, and empire-builders. Jesus summarized and dismissed the glory of Solomon with a single phrase: "Consider the lilies of the field, how they grow; they neither toil nor spin; yet I tell you, even Solomon in all his glory was not arrayed like one of these" (Matt. 6:28–29).

One might say, in fact, that two great themes run through the Bible, neither of which is comprehended in the worldly wisdom of Solomon, and neither of which managed to reach *The Blue Book of Social Usage*. On the one hand we have the theme of the greatness of the "one God and Father of us all, who is above all" (Eph. 4:6). It is a greatness that is above all worldly greatness, above all principalities and powers, above all empires and nations and private clubs, above all presidents and generals and business tycoons, above all heroes and superstars and matinee idols, above all corporate pyramids and social ladders and international conglomerates. Relative to *this* God all human beings and all human enterprises are as nothing, even the most successful and powerful and polished among us.

It was this message that was such a source of courage and strength to those who suffered under the successive waves of superpowers that overran part or all of Israel: Egypt, Assyria, Babylonia, Persia, Greece, Rome. Beyond the seemingly invincible might of the great empires of the day and the grandeur of their dazzling accomplishments was One, as Isaiah preached to the Babylonian exiles, before whom "the nations are like a drop from a bucket, and are accounted as the dust on the scales. . . . All the nations are as nothing before him, they are accounted by him as less than nothing and emptiness" (Isa. 40:15, 17).

All human wisdom and greatness are vanity to this One, "who brings princes to nought, and makes the rulers of the earth as nothing" (Isa. 40:23). Relative to this God the inhabitants of the earth are, as Isaiah put it, "like grasshoppers" before him. The difference between one human being and another, the differences about which we become so anxious and make so much fuss, are like so many fine distinctions in the small world of grasshoppers.

The other biblical theme, contradictory as it may seem, is that while the greatest is nothing before God, even the lowliest is of inestimable value in the sight of God. What has been taken away with one hand is given back with the other, freely and to all. In the first movement those that exalt themselves are humbled. In the second movement the humble are exalted. Because no one is of special importance before God, everyone is of special importance. In the Bible, people are singled out, not that they might be elevated one above another or because certain people are particularly worth singling out, but because each individual is of singular worth. Since "God is no respecter of persons," as the King James version puts it, all persons may be respected.

For this second theme the Bible shifts from the image of king to that of father or shepherd. To use Pauline phrasing, the one God who is "above all" is also "the one God and Father of us all." The God who is King above all kings, before whom even emperors and pharaohs are as nothing, is also the "Father of the fatherless" (Ps. 68:5). The great gulf between humanity and God, which annuls all human distinctions, is bridged by the love of God, which embraces even the weakest and lowliest.

This is the other side of Isaiah's message of hope to the exiles in Babylon. The power and glory of God are not to be compared with human power and glory. "To whom then will you compare me, that I should be like him? says the Holy One" (Isa. 40:25). God is not impressed by human importance and even less impressed by a self-importance that elevates itself above others. If anything, therefore, God is partial to the meek and oppressed. Because God is unmoved by human greatness, God is especially moved by human weakness. "He gives power to the faint, and to him who has no might he increases strength" (40:29).

Thus we are given that most paradoxical of affirmations:

> Behold, the Lord GOD comes with might,
>   and his arm rules for him. . . .
> He will feed his flock like a shepherd,
>   he will gather the lambs in his arms,
> he will carry them in his bosom,
>   and gently lead those that are with young.
>   (Isa. 40:10–11)

The same God who is "King of kings and Lord of lords" is also the gentle shepherd who walks with his sheep and tenderly takes in his arms the helpless and vulnerable.

Divine Inclusiveness

Human greatness is *exclusive*. Human beings are sorted out like eggs for the grading by the multitude of comparatives that are constantly employed in the secular world. People are ranked as rich or poor, intelligent or ignorant, beautiful or homely, worthy or unworthy, good or bad, or simply "we" or "they." Discrimination and discriminating taste are among the sterling achievements of worldly wisdom.

Divine greatness is *inclusive*. Before the reality that is truly ultimate, all human professions of goodness and claims to greatness are as nothing and vanity. The distinctions between lofty and lowly, courageous and cowardly, righteous and unrighteous are relativized. As in Jesus' parable of the vineyard, the laborers who were hired at the eleventh hour received the same pay as those hired at the third, sixth, and ninth hours (Matt. 20). Comparing the finite to the infinite is like comparing Volkswagens and Greyhound buses from the vantage point of the next galaxy; the differences are not very consequential. As Søren Kierkegaard put it:

> The claim to be the best man in the town of Kjøge is laughed at in Copenhagen, but to be the best man in Copenhagen is just as laughable. . . . He who turns against himself with the absolute standard will naturally not be able to live on in the blissful confidence that if he keeps the Commandments, and has never been convicted, and is regarded by a revivalistic clique as really a man of heart . . . [he] will in the course of time become all too perfect for this world.[5]

In this respect also the Bible advocates the comic perspective. In ancient Greek theater, while the tragedians were busily describing the noble deeds of divine and royal families (*Prometheus, Oedipus, Antigone*), the comedians responded by debunking important people (Socrates in *Clouds*) or making heroes of average people (*Lysistrata*) or representing humans as animals (*Birds, Frogs, Wasps*). Similarly, Shakespeare's tragedies dwelt on the affairs of a host of kings and queens, princes and princesses, noble lords and ladies: *Lear, Macbeth, John, Richard* (II and III), *Henry* (IV, V, VI, and VIII), *Othello, Julius Caesar, Antony and Cleopatra, Hamlet, Romeo and Juliet*. His comedies, on the other hand, belong more to the common people: *The Taming of the Shrew, The Merry Wives of Windsor, All's Well That Ends Well, As You Like It, Much Ado About Nothing*.

Theorists, from the time of Aristotle, have contended that tragedy imitates the actions of noble and superior people and that comedy imitates those who are common, inferior, or ignoble. In fact, Aristotle went so far as to classify tragedy with beauty and comedy with ugliness. Tragic action is sublime; comic action is ridiculous and ludicrous, which is a species of the ugly. What such classifications fail to note is that these are precisely the rankings that are being challenged in comedy. The consuming concern for nobility and superiority has in it something of the ludicrous and ridiculous, while the ludicrous and ridiculous may be found to contain something of the noble and sublime. As in the modern story of *The Elephant Man*, out of the most horrible deformities may shine forth the noblest of spirits.

Tragic literature defends elaborate social pyramids and is resolutely exclusive. Comic literature, on the other hand, is equalitarian and inclusive. The comedies confound and confuse the very distinctions that discriminate for and against people and that sort people into noble and ignoble. Beggars are invited to the banquet table; all workers are paid the same wages; privates behave like generals; fools are proclaimed king and queen for a day; the last person to cross the finish line receives the trophy; enemies are forgiven. The result of comedies is that people are brought together in a spirit of camaraderie; the result of tragedies is that people are pulled apart and alienated.

In Shakespearean comedy the most marginal and even roguish characters are, in the end, included rather than excluded. Caliban is given a reprieve in *The Tempest*; Falstaff is invited to the final feast in *The Merry Wives*; Angelo is allowed to live down his disgrace in *Measure for Measure*. As Northrop Frye has argued, *grace* is an important theme in the most mature comedies. The comic society conveys a strong sense of compassion and fellow feeling. The concern is not to maintain distinctions and distances—if necessary to the bitter end—but to overcome them. To enter such a society we must confess a common humanity and lay aside differences so that all may celebrate together. As Frye comments: "The tendency of the comic society to include rather than exclude is the reason for the traditional importance of the parasite, who has no business to be at the final festival but is nevertheless there."[6]

The Comic Society

In this sense the true comic society is the church. What other organization has a clause in its charter saying, "Whosoever will may come"? What other organization begins its assembly with a confession

of sin and develops a membership on the basis of a common sinfulness? What other organization invites its members to kneel or bow in a
posture of humility before God and one another? Although many
churches have practiced exclusivism relative to race or class or ethnic
origin or peculiarity of belief, to that extent they have failed to be
churches and have become instead religious clubs. In the church of
Christ:

> The eye cannot say to the hand, "I have no need of you," nor again the
> head to the feet, "I have no need of you." On the contrary, the parts of the
> body which seem to be weaker are indispensable, and those parts of the
> body which we think less honorable we invest with the greater honor. . . .
> If one member suffers, all suffer together; if one member is honored, all
> rejoice together. (1 Cor. 12:21–23, 26)

The one, seemingly glaring, exception to this inclusiveness and
equalitarian spirit is in the story of the Gentile woman who came to
Jesus to plead with him to cast a demon from her daughter. Here Jesus
seems to have used rather than challenged the discriminations between
Jew and Gentile. According to Matthew, Jesus "did not answer her a
word" (15:23) and when his disciples asked him to send her away, instead of rebuking the disciples as we might expect, Jesus remarked, "I
was sent only to the lost sheep of the house of Israel" (15:24). When
she persisted, Jesus responded further, "It is not fair to take the children's bread and throw it to the dogs" (15:26). Not to be denied, however, the woman quickly rejoined: "Yes, Lord, yet even the dogs eat
the crumbs that fall from their master's table" (15:27). Finally Jesus
acceded to her request: "O woman, great is your faith! Be it done for
you as you desire" (15:28). And her daughter was healed.

Although the end of the story is characteristic of Jesus, the beginning does not seem to be. Apparently Jesus had gone to the region of
Tyre and Sidon to rest, since Matthew says that he "withdrew to the
district" (15:21) and Mark says that he "entered a house, and would
not have any one know it" (7:24). Jesus seems to have been weary and
to have wanted to be left alone. Many crowds of people for some time
had pressed upon him with their cries for help. Considering his desire
to retreat and to remain incognito, Jesus' initial response is understand-
able. When she insists, even hounding the disciples, who in turn complain to Jesus, Jesus puts her off by saying that he "was sent only to

the lost sheep of the house of Israel'' (Matt. 15:24). The situation may be likened to that of a doctor tending the wounded behind battle lines: pressed to the limit of his resources in caring for the soldiers of his regiment, he may yet be persuaded, under extreme circumstance, to give aid to a civilian.

When the Syrophoenician woman persists and demonstrates her faith by her persistence, Jesus has compassion on her and lays aside his personal exhaustion and his desire to be alone. If Jesus was testing her with his responses, she proved herself by her perseverance, even to the point of offering Jesus a quick-witted rejoinder to his statement about giving children's bread to the dogs: "even the dogs eat the crumbs that fall from their master's table" (Matt. 15:27). Jesus may well have smiled at the wit of that exchange. Jesus knew that he was dealing with a woman who could not lightly be denied. Even though he saw his ministry as directed to the "lost sheep of the house of Israel," his compassionate dealings with Gentiles and Samaritans set in motion a spirit that has proved capable of breaking down all barriers and discriminations. In that spirit the social distinctions between slave and free, rich and poor, king and peasant, and the ethnic distinctions between Jew and Samaritan or Jew and Gentile are overcome.

The comic gospel often seems idealistic and irrelevant and unworkable in the real world. Only someone who does not know how the real world operates could propose such utopianisms. How could the comic gospel possibly be applied to the world of aggressive advertising, cutthroat competition, stock investment, social climbing, racial or international strife? Is it not so much divine foolishness?

Still, the comic gospel does sometimes break through into the real world. In the forties and fifties the daily broadcasts of a well-known radio commentator were heard by millions of listeners in the United States and many foreign countries. From such an audience he of course received a great deal of correspondence, so much that several secretaries were needed to sort each day's mail. From it they would select the few most important letters from the few most important people; to these he would have the time and inclination to make a personal response. The rest of the letters would be answered with a form letter or simply discarded.

One day an unusual letter caught a secretary's attention. It was not unusual in the sense of being outstanding or from an outstanding person. Just the opposite. The letter was from someone of no consequence in a remote part of the country. It was very poorly written, filled with misspelled words and incorrect grammar, and in the shaky handwriting of an elderly writer. The secretary thought the commentator might find it amusing.

The letter was written by a man who said that he was a shepherd in the hills of North Dakota. His wife had died many years earlier. His children were grown and had moved to distant places. His nearest neighbor was some twenty miles away. His only companions were a dog, a radio, and a violin. The radio was his main contact with the outside world. It was clear from the letter that he thought of the radio commentator, whom he had listened to for years, as an old acquaintance.

The reason he was writing the letter was that his violin had gotten out of tune. He had turned to his friend. He wondered whether some day the commentator on his national radio broadcast would play an A on the piano so that he could get his violin back in tune!

Normally such a letter would have been discarded. At best it would have been answered with a form letter. But one day, right in the midst of a nationwide broadcast, right in the midst of a commentary on the most important world affairs, right in the midst of the names of presidents and generals and star athletes, there was a pause.

"Shepherd of the North Dakota hills, are you listening? Shepherd of the North Dakota hills, are you listening?" Then a note was struck loudly and clearly on the piano. "This is your A. This is your A."

If only for a moment, the ways of the world were interrupted and its conventional wisdom challenged. If only for a moment one of the oddly assorted frumps on the outskirts of polite society was invited to the party and given a place of special prominence.

6

Miracles
in
Common
Places

To me the meanest flower that blows can give
Thoughts that do often lie too deep for tears.

—William Wordsworth
"Ode on Intimations of Immortality"

If one of the great biblical themes is the comic theme that God is to be
found among humble people, a parallel theme is that God is also to be
found in humble places. Although human wisdom would look for God
in the palaces and temples of worldly imagination, God is as likely to
be found in the mangers and carpenter shops of our lives. The God of
the common people is also the God of common places.

The figure of the fifteenth-century French heroine Joan of Arc combines both religious themes. George Bernard Shaw, in his play *Saint
Joan*, captures the scenario well. Joan is but a peasant maid from a
small French village who has claimed to have visions from God calling
her to help the French in their fight against invading English armies.
She has undertaken to lead and inspire French troops, despite the fact
that she is a woman, a young woman in fact, of but eighteen years. She
has done so, furthermore, quite apart from the authority of the crown or
the nobility or the military or the church.

Joan has been summoned before King Charles VII. The king has commanded her to explain how she, but a peasant maid, has had the audacity to involve herself in the war with England and by whose authority she has taken it upon herself to marshal troops and take them into battle. Innocently but boldly, Joan stands alone before the king, surrounded by courtiers, soldiers, nobles, and church officials. Bravely she tells the king how she has felt God's presence in many places and has heard, as it were, God speaking to her and compelling her to help her country in its time of crisis. The weakling King Charles interrupts impatiently: "O your voices, your voices! Why don't the voices come to me? *I* am the King of France, not you!"

Joan calmly replies: "They do come to you; but you do not hear them. You have not sat in the field in the evening listening for them. When the angelus rings you cross yourself and have done with it; but if you prayed from your heart, and listened to the thrilling of the bells in the air after they stop ringing, you would hear the voices as well as I do."[1]

The House of God

If one may generalize about the lives of the saints of the church, what they seem to have had in common is a strong sense of the reality and power of God. They have been sensitive to the presence, the nearness, the here and nowness of God. God has become to them, in Tennyson's words, "closer . . . than breathing, and nearer than hands and feet." They have been engaged—in the words of an older devotional manual—in *The Practice of the Presence of God.*

As the title of the little book by Brother Lawrence suggests, this sensitivity requires some practice! Yet where is God present and the presence of God to be practiced? In ancient Israel it was commonly understood, particularly from a priestly point of view, that God was specially and primarily present in Jerusalem: in the temple, which was the house of God, and more specifically in the holy of Holies. The temple was where one practiced the presence of God, and one did so by prescribed rituals and appointed sacrifices.

In the book of Jonah, when Jonah hears the command of God to preach to Nineveh—and promptly runs off in the opposite direction—

the text refers to this three times as "fleeing from the presence of God." Jonah is represented as imagining that if he got far enough out into the Mediterranean, God could not reach him and the Word of God could not be heard.

Jonah's theology is like that of the small girl in one of the anecdotes attributed to Mark Twain. Her parents were moving from the East Coast to Missouri. She stood wistfully in the front yard of their New England home, saying her last good-byes. "Good-bye house," she said tearfully, "We're going to Missouri." Turning to the stately trees in the front yard, she said, "Good-bye trees, we're going to Missouri." Looking down at the lawn on which she had romped and played, she said, "Good-bye grass, we're going to Missouri." Then with one last gesture she looked up at the sky and said, "Well, good-bye God, we're going to Missouri."

Such was Jonah's view as he said good-bye to the God of the land of Canaan and the temple in Jerusalem and set off for Tarshish. This understanding and sense of the presence of God is a common one still—and we often complain about it as "Sunday-go-to-meeting" religion. The very existence of holy places and sacred rituals and ordained officiants tends to encourage and confirm this emphasis on the "cultic presence" of God. Where is God to be found? God's presence is to be experienced, God's Word to be heard, God's worship to be offered, in "God's house": in the most sublime and most sacred place of our lives. Here God is somehow more real and available than anywhere else, and we are certainly more presentable to God—well behaved, well dressed, well groomed, clean-shaven, amply perfumed, and recently bathed as we are!

Such a view was decisively challenged by the Apostle Paul in his sermon to the Athenians. Surrounded by the temples and altars of the Parthenon, he declared unto them the one God, "who made the world and everything in it." This God, argued Paul, "being Lord of heaven and earth, does not live in shrines made by man, nor is he served by human hands, as though he needed anything, since he himself gives to all men life and breath and everything. . . . He is not far from each one of us, for 'In him we live and move and have our being. . . .' " (Acts 17:24–28). In other words the whole universe is God's house, and we are the invited guests. There is nowhere to live and move and have our being except in God's house.

Even when we go beyond a God's-house mentality, we tend to perpetuate a similar problem, outside the church and its rituals. If we look for God beyond the sanctuary, we continue to look in *special* places, *extraordinary* events, *dramatic* moments, *sublime* circumstances, *peak* experiences. God is present in places of unusual power and prominence, theophanies of greatness.

This association of God with superlative events was, at best, as far as Jonah's understanding got beyond the cultic presence of God in Jerusalem. God reached him out there in the Mediterranean by throwing a *great* wind and *great* storm at him, by sending a *great* fish to transport him, and by *miraculously* preserving him from drowning and from being dissolved in the belly of the fish. There had certainly been no sense of the presence of God before the storm, in the gentle breezes and blue sky and soft lapping of the waves.

We are presented with a similar situation in the story of Moses and the burning bush. Moses is out on the backside of the desert, tending sheep, far removed from the problems of fellow Israelites in Egypt—as we might say, out of town, on vacation, with no phone, and unreachable. God, however, attracts Moses' attention by means of a burning bush that miraculously is not consumed. Why? Because now and then God has to do something extraordinary to get our attention.

We should not conclude, however, as we so easily do, that God is to be found only in mighty tempests and burning bushes and not in the common, everyday events of life. As Saint Joan put it: "When the angelus rings you cross yourself and have done with it; but if you prayed from your heart, and listened to the thrilling of the bells in the air after they stop ringing, you would hear the voices as well as I do."

So often we think of the presence of God in terms of holy places, supernatural occurrences, soul-shaking experiences, great emotional highs, signs and wonders, special miracles, with the result that vast regions of our lives are emptied of any sense of the presence of God—as if God were not also to be found in ordinary places, as if God were restricted to the more obvious places, as if there were not something very unusual and quite miraculous about everything that surrounds us.

As the poet Minot Savage wrote:

> In wonder workings, or some bush aflame,
> Men look for God and fancy Him concealed;
> But in earth's common things He stands revealed.
> ("Earth's Common Things")

There are those in evangelical and charismatic circles who circulate from religious meeting to religious meeting, trying to receive or revive some climactic religious experience. Spirituality is understood as a matter of capturing and recapturing fleeting moments of religious ecstasy. Yet surely God is not limited to such moments. While we are waiting to hear the thundering voice of God from the shrouded heights of Mount Sinai, we may miss the still small voice of God that whispers from so many unnoticed places in the valley below.

Elizabeth Barrett Browning also wrote a poem on Moses and the burning bush. For her the issue was not the absence or the remoteness of God, but the lack of human sensitivity.

> Earth is crammed with heaven,
> And every common bush afire with God;
> But only he who sees takes off his shoes,
> The rest sit round it and pluck blackberries.
> ("Aurora Leigh")

Overcoming the Secular

Two movements characterize the religious life. One is the separation of the sacred from the profane. We build our holy places, we reenact sacred rituals, we maintain an ordained priesthood, we use consecrated vessels, we read from inspired texts, we sing religious songs, we recite hallowed creeds. This spirituality understands the sacred as the sphere that is set apart from the secular world and that must be preserved from contamination by profane hands. In this holy ground are to be found the sacred places and objects that radiate special power and blessing.

Such a view tends to turn sanctuaries and priesthoods, crosses and communion sets, into holy relics to be revered and approached in fear and trembling. It is not so different from the accumulation and veneration of relics throughout Europe in the Middle Ages, which Luther so roundly criticized: a tooth of John the Baptist, a piece of thread from Jesus' swaddling cloth, straw from the manger, a strand of Christ's beard, a crumb of bread from the Last Supper, slivers of wood from the cross, a twig from Moses' burning bush, a drop of milk from Mother Mary. As Luther once quipped, the Archbishop of Mainz, not to be outdone, claimed to have two feathers and an egg from the Holy Ghost!

The other movement in the religious life is the opposite of the first. It is the *overcoming* of the sharp distinction between sacred and profane things. It is the return to this everyday, ordinary world with renewed fascination and marvel. The presence and the power of God are found in the most ordinary places and things. We are struck with the sense that nothing stands outside God. God is seen as the infinite circumference of all things. As Paul added in his sermon to the Athenians, "In him we live and move and have our being."

From this standpoint we need holy places to remind us that God is everyplace. We need sacred rites to remind us that all life is sacred. We need divine miracles to remind us that all existence is a miracle. We need God incarnate, Emmanuel, "God with us," to remind us that God is always with us. "Whither shall I go from thy Spirit, or whither shall I flee from thy presence?" exclaims the psalmist (Ps. 139:7).

J.B. Phillips once wrote a devotional book with the provocative title, *Your God Is Too Small.* Isn't that part of our problem? Though we, like Jonah, profess to believe in the one God Almighty, Maker of heaven and earth, do we not tend to believe in a lesser god who is but a pale, shrunken shadow of such a God? Our belief is much like the words of Elizabeth Burrows' parody: "I want a simple, friendly god, above a near and friendly sky. I want him to be wise, of course, but not too much wiser than I."

Yet is there any place of which it can fully and finally be said, "God is not here; God cannot work here; God does not speak here; God could not surprise us here"? Is there any place that can exclude God totally or that God totally excludes, a place that is completely godless or godforsaken? If we really believe, with Paul, that God is not only "above all" but "through all and in all" and that all things are "in him" (Eph. 4:6), then no place is completely devoid of God's presence and activity. In no situation can we say confidently: "God cannot confront us here; God has nothing to say to us here."

The God of the Bible is the God who can make even the "wrath of men to praise him"; who can bring wisdom out of the mouths of babes; who can, if need be, call upon stones to cry out; who can work the divine pleasure through Cyrus, king of Persia, as well as Isaiah, prophet of Israel; who can speak through the mouth of Balaam's ass as well as Balaam the seer.

Remember Tennyson's words in "Flower in the Crannied Wall"?

> I pluck you out of the crannies;
> Hold you here, root and all, in my hand,
> Little flower—but if I could understand
> What you are, root and all, and all in all,
> I should know what God and man is.

The real test of religious experience is not whether we can find God in the obvious places, the sublime moments, the grand vistas, the ecstatic experiences, but whether we can find God in the simple ordinary, taken-for-granted circumstances of our lives, and there sense the divine presence and mystery. After all, even the tiniest and most insignificant wildflower is an unfathomable mystery. We do not need to pluck the flower out of the cranny and place it on a church altar to sense within it, root and all, a divine immanence.

The Protestant reformers were very critical of the worldliness of the clergy and church of their day, advocating a renewal of spirituality and godliness. In another sense, however, the reformers took spirituality out of the monastery and the sanctuary and brought it back into the world. In so doing, Protestantism rediscovered the world and recovered its religious meaning. The world was seen as spiritualized and sanctified by virtue of the grace of creation, incarnation, and justification. The world of flesh and matter was not to be looked down upon as the lower regions of the spirit, nor was the sphere of lay persons and secular vocations beneath that of "the religious" and their religious practices.

Luther left the monastery and married a former nun and presumably, therefore, left a religious life for a secular life. Eventually, as one thing led to another, Martin and Katerina had children. Yet even before

his marriage and family life, Luther had begun to develop a very different understanding of the relationship between the religious and the secular. Notice how Luther interpreted the utterly mundane world of
rocking and burping and bathing and clothing babies. The following is
from Luther's treatise "The Estate of Marriage" (1522):

> Now observe that when that clever harlot, our natural reason . . . takes a
> look at married life, she turns up her nose and says, "Alas, must I rock the
> baby, wash its diapers, make its bed, smell its stench, stay up nights with
> it, take care of it when it cries, heal its rashes and sores, and on top of that
> care for my wife, provide for her, labor at my trade, take care of this and
> take care of that, do this and do that, endure this and endure that, and what-
> ever else of bitterness and drudgery married life involves? What, should I
> make such a prisoner of myself? . . . It is better to remain free and lead a
> peaceful, carefree life; I will become a priest or a nun and compel my chil-
> dren to do likewise."
>
>   What then does Christian faith say to this? It opens its eyes, looks upon
> all these insignificant, distasteful, and despised duties in the Spirit, and is
> aware that they are all adorned with divine approval as with the costliest
> gold and jewels. It says, "O God, because I am certain that thou hast cre-
> ated me as a man and hast from my body begotten this child, I also know
> for a certainty that it meets with thy perfect pleasure. I confess to thee that I
> am not worthy to rock the little babe or wash its diapers, or to be entrusted
> with the care of the child and its mother. How is it that I, without any
> merit, have come to this distinction of being certain that I am serving thy
> creature and thy most precious will? O how gladly will I do so, though the
> duties should be even more insignificant and despised. Neither frost nor
> heat, neither drudgery nor labor, will distress or dissuade me, for I am cer-
> tain that it is thus pleasing in thy sight."[2]

Is this caring for infants not also a divine folly? Who but God has
created the foolishness of all these dull, daily tasks that children represent—that children literally are—the foolishness of infant gibberish,
the gurgling and gooing and cooing, the broad smiles over the simplest
pleasures and the loud cries of protest over the smallest discomforts? Is
this not part of the divine comedy of creation, this returning for the tril-
lionth time to the same elementary movements, the learning of everything all over again in an endless round of fresh starts, yet each time as
if for the very first time? In that tiny gift of life are concentrated the
mystery and the wonder of being itself.

The Recovery of Wonder

Several years ago a former Catholic priest, Ken Feit, wandered about the country as an itinerant fool. He listed himself on his calling card and signed his correspondence, "Ken Feit, Fool." Many people are fools, of course, but not many are willing to admit it publicly. Ken was interested in reviving the medieval fool tradition because he believed that some important perceptions in that tradition had been lost. He had remained a Catholic but had left the priesthood to devote his time to performing "fool's rituals." The objective of the rituals was to take the symbolism of the sacred out of the church and into the world.

One of his "fool's rituals" was the Paper Bag Mass. He would sit cross-legged on the ground or on the floor of a gym or on the carpeting of a lounge—wherever. He would gather about him in a semicircle, also sitting cross-legged, his "congregation"—whoever. He was barefoot and wore a white undershirt and blue jeans, for this was to be a liturgy that sanctified ordinary things. He applied the whiteface that authorized him to officiate as the fool-priest of the ritual.

The ritual begins in silence, for in silence one may be able better to sense the presence of God in those things that do not so obviously and conventionally announce God's presence or speak God's word. The fool-priest sets before him an old brown paper bag, filled with peculiar objects: a banana, an apple, a balloon, a lump of clay, paper and scissors, a needle and thread. The ritual consists of taking these objects out of the bag, one by one. A look of expectancy is on the fool's face as he reaches into the bag, like a small child opening a birthday present or like an infant seeing objects for the first time.

He takes out the banana. He jerks back in surprise. His eyes open wide in amazement. The congregation, still in silent wonder, round their mouths in a pantomimed "Wow!" Bananas really are strange and curious things. The fool cautiously scrutinizes the banana. He sniffs it and touches it gingerly and finally makes bold to pinch it. It starts to peel. He pulls on it, and it peels some more. He ventures a nibble, and his eyes light up in delight.

The ordinary world is not very ordinary after all. Its ordinariness is only a sign that our sensitivities have become dulled. Bananas no longer jump out at us and surprise us. The problem is not with the banana, but with us. The banana is just as odd, amazing, marvelous, and mysterious as ever. But we have grown accustomed to bananas—and in like manner we tend systematically to empty vast regions of our experience of their intrinsic wonderment.

Our situation is well described by the Welsh poet Huw Menai:

> If the good God were suddenly
> To make a solitary Blind to see
> We would stand wondering all
> And call it a miracle;
> But that He gives with lavish hand
> Sight to a million souls we stand
> And say, with little awe,
> He but fulfills a natural law!
>   ("Paradox")

There is a delightful old story of a Chinese monk named Yao-shan, who lived in a monastery near the top of a mountain. In the evenings it was his habit to take a stroll around the monastery before retiring. One cloudy evening, as he was taking his walk, the full moon suddenly appeared from behind the clouds. The monk was so surprised that he began laughing uproariously. He laughed so loudly, in fact, that his laughter was heard many miles away in the village in the valley below, awakening the villagers from their slumbers. The next day the villagers were inquiring among themselves as to who had been carousing the night before and making such a commotion. Unable to find anyone in the village at fault, the villagers concluded that "the master gave us the greatest laugh of his life at the top of the mountain."[3]

The point of the story is that Yao-shan, no doubt, had seen the moon innumerable times. Yet for the first time he had really seen the moon. Instead of a matter-of-fact, mere noticing acquaintance with the moon, this time he suddenly realized the magic, the marvel, the mystery that was this moon. In that moment it was no longer simply the same old familiar moon. The moon had jumped out at him, had surprised him, had ambushed him from behind the clouds. It was as if the moon were suddenly ablaze with the same fire that lighted Moses' burning bush. In that simple experience the whole mystery of being and the wondrousness of existence opened up before him. He laughed and exclaimed with joy, "How marvelous, how marvelous, the moon!"

The great enemy of religion is not godlessness so much as matter-of-factness, not the spirit of some defiant antichrist but spiritlessness. After all, rebellion against God at least has some spunk and passion to it. But what is one to do with apathy, dullness, passivity, boredom? There are those for whom life is alive and ringing with great wonders and those for whom life is largely a ho-hum parade of trivia. Instead of a world filled with incredible creations—like the childhood marvels on Old McDonald's farm, with a pig, goat, horse, cow, chicken, duck, and goose here, there, and everywhere—it becomes for many a world of blah: "Here blah, there blah, everywhere blah, blah!"

The situation is analogous to the basic problem in education: the lack of fascination. The reason things get studied at all is that, in the first place, they have been fascinating to someone. Their very existence has caused someone to wonder and draw closer "to see this thing which is come to pass." The great enemy of education is not "invincible ignorance" but indifference. When the spirit "Who cares?" reigns, education is reduced to note taking, regardless of how many wonders are unveiled or how many burning bushes are trotted out. Learning is turned into a collection of odd bits of information, strung together into a skeletal outline of dead facts and memorized through various mnemonic devices for the purpose of passing examinations.

The basic question common to religion and education is this: In this world of scintillating objects, ideas, and events jumping out from all directions and in all shapes and sizes, when is the last time you said "Wow!"? Both religion and education are fundamentally an awakening of a profound sense of mystery. We are drawn beyond the mere noticing of the moon or the banana, the bells and the blackberry bushes. We become fascinated by a world suddenly afire and alive and amazingly present. Both religion and education are constantly threatened by those who do not see any burning bushes or hear the thrilling of the bells, who never stop to exclaim in wonder, who are neither amazed nor amused, who are not even moved to say "Really?"

Wonder is not commonly thought of as a religious virtue. Honesty, of course; faith, to be sure; hope, certainly; love, by all means. But wonder? Actually, though, wonder is one of the more fundamental religious virtues, perhaps the most fundamental of all. Religion arises out of a sense of wonder. After all, animals do not wonder; people do. The cows may wonder when they are going to be fed. The dog may wonder when you are going to let him in the back door. But only people wonder about the origin of the universe or the meaning of life or whether there is life after death. Only people look up at the moon and the stars, the mountains and the clouds, with a sense of mystery and awe. Only people ponder the wings of birds and the petals of flowers and the webs of spiders and are amazed. A monkey may wonder about the promised reward of a banana; it is people who wonder about bananas.

Nothing is exempt from this human marveling. The sense of wonder is evoked not only in relation to stupendous occurrences and extraordinary phenomena but in relation to every object and event in our experience. Wonder is central to human consciousness. Yet, like any of the physical senses, wonder may be dulled by repeated experiences of the same thing. The sensitivity to the wonder of all things has to be kept fresh and alive. Like any virtue, wonder must be cultivated. We do this, however, not by searching for the supernatural or unusual, but by rediscovering the supernatural in the natural and the unusual in the ordinary. As Walt Whitman put it, "Even a mouse is mystery enough to stagger sextillions of infidels."

7

The
Day
Jonah
Swallowed
the
Whale

When I was a seminary student, I was once asked to lead a midweek
Bible study in my home church on the book of Jonah. I decided to begin in a lighthearted manner with the "great fish" appointed to swallow Jonah. Though this is hardly the main concern of the book,
attention has often been centered on the question whether there were
any whales large enough—and interested enough—to swallow a full-
grown man and whether, if so, there was a man tough enough to be
able to survive three days in the belly of such a whale without being
asphyxiated or dissolved in the gastric juices. To all this wonderment I
added, further, the question whether Jonah, had he been able by sheer
grit or orneriness to have survived, would have been in any condition
to walk the next 600 miles to Nineveh and preach. I then remarked
that, since these issues were not the point of the book anyway, it didn't
really matter whether the whale swallowed Jonah or Jonah swallowed
the whale.

I soon discovered that, to most of my audience, it mattered. Only
three people managed polite smiles; the rest sat in hostile silence. They
had expected that I was leading them to a proof that this series of
events could and did happen, that the Bible offers the story as a historical report on several divine miracles, and that the story is the verbatim

biography of a very disobedient prophet named Jonah. They heard little I had to say beyond that point about the religious message of the book as an affirmation of the foolishness of divine grace.

One of the results of this experience was that I became convinced that God had not called me to become a stand-up comic. I was not, however, dissuaded from my conviction that humor is an important part of biblical literature, of preaching, and of the Christian life. Nor was I shaken in my belief that the book of Jonah is a unique book that has been much misunderstood because interpreters have assumed it to be a historical treatise and thus gotten inordinately involved in speculations about the mouths and stomachs of whales. I have also remained convinced that a measure of this uniqueness is that there is considerable humor in the book, a large part of which is the comic portrait of a messenger who was willing to do anything to avoid delivering his message to the Ninevites. Jonah, in fact, if it had been possible, would have swallowed the whale if that could have kept him from going to Nineveh.

The Unprophetic Prophet

Clearly enough, the book of Jonah is an unusual book. Though located among the seventeen prophetic books, Jonah contains no prophecies or preachings, except for a brief pronouncement: "Yet forty days, and Nineveh shall be overthrown"—a prediction that does not come true. The book of Jonah does not look like the other prophetic books, replete as they are with extensive visions and preachments yet with minimal historical and biographical information. The book is entirely devoted to the tale of an unwilling, uncooperative, and unmerciful messenger who refuses to deliver his message until coerced into doing so.

Jonah also does not look like any of the Hebrew prophets, and nowhere is he specifically referred to as a prophet. Although he is not depicted as a false prophet, he is nevertheless quite different from Amos or Isaiah or Jeremiah or Ezekiel—even the lesser prophets, such as Habakkuk, Haggai, and Obadiah. The very unprophetic character of the book and its "prophet" ought at least to arouse the suspicion that this material may require special canons of interpretation. Indeed, the location of such an unprophetic prophet and unprophetic book in the prophetic literature rather than among the historical books in itself suggests that the story is not properly classified as history.

If Jonah is a prophetic book, it must be because the prophetic message of the book is the story as such. The real prophet is the *writer* of the book of Jonah, who is offering this story as his prophetic deliverance. He is like the prophet Nathan, who appeared before the errant king David to tell him a rather innocent-sounding story (of the rich and poor shepherds), leading to David's unwitting self-judgment. Nathan had only to say: "Thou art the man!"

The book of Jonah does not begin by informing us what kind of narrative literature it is. That silence, though, should not be taken to imply that the book is therefore historical and biographical, given the many possibilities within narrative literature. Since satire and irony were established prophetic devices, those options can hardly be ruled out. In fact, they are much more likely, considering the many peculiarities of the book and its placement among the prophetic books.

The oft-cited observation that Jesus refers to the story of Jonah— "For as Jonah was three days and three nights in the belly of the whale, so will the Son of man be three days and three nights in the heart of the earth" (Matt. 12:40)—does not prove the historicity of the story. Such a reference may imply no more than a comparison with an episode from a familiar story. If a modern writer, for example, were to refer to an incident in *Hamlet* or *Othello* as precedent for a contemporary situation, we would not take the reference as proof that the person believed these plays to be biographies or historical treatises.

In its biblical context the figure of Jonah could not have been used as a historical account of an unparalleled prophetic event, the total conversion of the populace of the pagan city of Nineveh and its preservation from destruction. No corroborative evidence has been found within or without the Bible for any such conversion. A prophet named Jonah is mentioned in 2 Kings 14:25 in the time of Jeroboam. Yet if the book of Jonah is his biography, it credits his ministry with results that are the *opposite* of what actually occurred, since Nineveh—during or shortly after the historical Jonah's lifetime—instead of repenting and being converted, swept down and conquered Israel. The Assyrian archives make no mention of any dramatic religious changes; rather, they present a consistent pattern of military activity and worship of the gods and goddesses of the Assyrian pantheon. Nineveh, furthermore, was not finally saved from destruction but was destroyed by the Babylonians in 612 B.C.

Everyone in the immediate audience of the book of Jonah would have known this: that the Ninevites, far from undergoing a moral and religious transformation, were the people of the capital city of the Assyrian empire, which had devastated Jewish cities, killing many of its people, deporting much of the surviving population, and bringing in non-Jewish peoples from other conquered areas of the empire (2 Kings 17). This knowledge is precisely the basis for the satire that is now going to be told, preposterous though it may be historically. In fact, the account is much more workable as a satire because of its preposterousness. No foreign city or people had been despised as had Nineveh and the Assyrians. The author of Jonah could not have chosen more unlikely and undeserving recipients of divine grace. Nineveh offered the most extreme—and therefore ideal—test case for the ethical and theological issues with which the book of Jonah is concerned. The prophetic charge given to Jonah to preach to the Ninevites provides the supreme measure of Jewish attitudes and opinions on these issues. It also provides the supreme measure of divine mercy and forgiveness.[1]

A Comic Satire

A careful perusal of the story of Jonah, and of the differences between Jonah and other prophets and prophetic books, suggests that the story is not only a satire but a *comic* satire. The comic aspects of the story have been observed for some time. James D. Smart, for example, in *The Interpreter's Bible*, does not specifically identify the book of Jonah as a comic satire, but he points to various comic features that could have led him to this conclusion. He notes the prominence of "inconsistency," "absurdity, one might also say idiocy" in the behavior of Jonah. He observes that the story uses "caricature" and at times a "grim humor," even that the "picture of Jonah in chs. 3–4 is ludicrous in the extreme." Having called attention to these various hallmarks of a comic literature, Smart comes as close as one could come to identifying the story as a comedy without actually doing so, perhaps because the traditional assumptions about biblical materials have not included comedy as an option.[2]

All the specific aspects of the book of Jonah, however, point to its having been developed intentionally as a comic satire. In the comical person and behavior of a totally uncooperative prophet are satirized a variety of evils that we associate with pride, prejudice, narrow-mindedness, stubbornness, exclusivism, selfishness, animosity, and hypocrisy. What is central to the tale, in fact, is a comic portrayal of the biblical theme of human wisdom and divine foolishness.

Jonah upholds a conventional sense of justice in which the hated Ninevites deserve "to get what's coming to them," without warning and without mercy. Has God not said that "the way of the wicked will perish" (Ps. 1:6)? Jonah wants nothing short of retaliation and revenge for the havoc the Assyrian imperialistic ambitions have wrought in the Middle East. Anything less would be a mockery of justice and fair play. They have sinned enormously, and they should pay in like measure for their sins. "An eye for an eye, and a tooth for a tooth." The idea that they should be warned of their impending destruction (forty days even!) seems to Jonah a pointless exercise that can only give them a chance to prepare for, or try to avoid, the disaster. Even more repugnant to Jonah's sensitivities is the chance that, given ample warning, they might plead for mercy. Then God, who has had a reputation in the past for being an easy touch and given to changing his mind, might become "soft on Nineveh" and spare them. That, for Jonah, would be the ultimate in divine foolishness.

The book of Jonah, whatever its historical merit, is written as a comic tale and uses a considerable range of comic devices aimed at demonstrating the contradictions in Jonah's position. Jonah maintains to the bitter end a *tragic* view of human relationships: there is to be no reconciliation between God and Nineveh or between Israel and Nineveh. All of Jonah's behavior is premised on this. The writer of the book of Jonah, on the other hand, holds this view up for critique, in fact ridicule, and offers a *comic* view of human relationships. In this comic view, though Nineveh has done great evil against Israel and before God and though Nineveh deserves vengeance and destruction, there is a higher and nobler level of relationships. On this higher plane Nineveh may be forgiven by God and by Israel. On this higher plane, compassion and magnanimity, repentance and reconciliation, are possible.

Jonah's arguments are very persuasive, and we, too, have often been persuaded by similar arguments relative to our own adversaries and enemies. The result of Jonah's attempt to stand uncompromisingly by his principles, however, is that it is Jonah, not God, who looks foolish. Again and again in the story Jonah's wisdom turns into folly, his simple justice becomes injustice, and his self-righteousness falls into hypocrisy.

One of the more effective ways of getting at such issues is not to preach them directly but to approach them indirectly through irony, satire, and humor. Comedy offers a subtler method. It sneaks up on us unawares. Or, to switch the metaphor, it comes after us with well-baited hooks. When we look at the figure of Jonah, his self-centeredness and narrow-mindedness, his extreme behavior, his self-contradictions, we laugh at him and, as we laugh, realize that we are laughing at ourselves.

Throughout the book of Jonah, the devices used are the stock-in-trade of comedy: overstatement, understatement, surprise, opposite reaction, inconsistency, inappropriate response, ludicrous behavior, absurdity. We are led thereby to realize that in the course of being entertained by such devices, we have been tried and convicted. Our laughter at Jonah becomes a judgment on ourselves. In enjoying his wisdom turning into foolishness, we discover in the comic mirror the foolishness of our own wisdom. This is the genius of great comedy, and the book of Jonah is one of the world's greatest and earliest comedies. If we get the point of the comedy at all, we hear the still, small voice within, saying, "Thou art the man."

To get the full effect of the opening comic device of an "opposite reaction," we must recall the geography of the story. Nineveh was to the northeast of Israel, whereas Tarshish (probably present-day Spain) was commonly believed to be the farthest point west. When the divine command comes to preach to the Ninevites, Jonah's immediate response is to proceed as rapidly as possible in the opposite direction: "Jonah rose to flee to Tarshish from the presence of the LORD. He went down to Joppa and found a ship going to Tarshish" (1:3). Note also what Jonah did *not* do. He did not respond as a prophet should respond: "Here am I, LORD, send me." No, when the Word of the Lord came, Jonah got out of there as fast as his little legs would carry him!

His reaction is even more extreme if one considers that the initial charge was not to convert the city or to seek some compromise or reconciliation but simply to "cry out" against it; "for their wickedness has come up before me" (1:2). Who in Israel could have objected to such a message, for it was surely what everyone in Israel had cried out against Nineveh? Jonah, of course, later explains that, as much as he might have enjoyed denouncing Nineveh and seeing the city destroyed, he had been afraid that they might repent of their sins and then God might have had mercy on them. Presumably Jonah would have proceeded directly to Nineveh, without question or complaint, if he could have been guaranteed that the city would be destroyed. But he has misgivings about God's peculiar sense of justice and reputation for changeability, similar to the complaint of the people in Malachi 3:14, 15.

> "It is vain to serve God. What is the good of our keeping his charge or of walking as in mourning before the LORD of hosts? Henceforth we deem the arrogant blessed; evildoers not only prosper but when they put God to the test they escape."

Jonah is also depicted from the first as involved in two related self-contradictions that are part of the movement and the message of the story. Jonah reflects the tensions in Israel between a tribal and a cosmic view of God, and correspondingly between a parochial and a universal vision of humanity. Three times it is said in the first chapter that Jonah was fleeing from "the presence of the LORD" (1:2, 3, 10). Now, in one sense, this is standard terminology for the cultic presence of God in Israel, especially in the temple in Jerusalem. Yet it is precisely that strong sense of the special presence and work of God in Israel that could become the denial of the possibility of God's special presence and work anywhere else. God's compassion and grace bestowed upon the Hebrews could easily be seen as exclusive of compassion and grace for anyone else, least of all for the wicked Ninevites.

Even the pagan sailors in the story, who in several ways are shown to be much more exemplary than Jonah, pray to God as one specially present in the storm and immediately available to their supplication.

When Jonah finally resorts to prayer from the belly of the fish, he prays as one who imagines God to be far away, residing in the temple at Jerusalem (2:7). Presumably, in Jonah's mind, God's presence hovered primarily over Israel and was accessible only through the temple. Thus if Jonah could make a fast enough getaway and escape some distance into the Mediterranean (certainly if he could get to Tarshish), God could no longer reach him. He could pass the rest of his days well out of range of divine commands and without fear of extradition, along the Spanish Riviera!

When God sends a storm after Jonah's escape vessel and the sailors begin crying out "each . . . to his god," even throwing the cargo overboard to keep the ship from sinking, where is Jonah? He is down in the hold of the ship, fast asleep. Jonah is supremely confident that he has made his getaway from the presence of God, clear of conscience in his refusal to obey the Word of the Lord and comfortable in his belief that God has no business being exercised over the Ninevites! While the ship is being dashed about and everyone else is frantically rushing to lighten the ship of its cargo, Jonah is sleeping as peacefully as a baby rocked in its cradle!

On the other hand, when lots are cast to determine on whose account the evil had come upon the voyagers and the lot falls on Jonah, he begins his explanation by claiming to believe in "the God of heaven, who made the sea and the dry land" (1:9). If so, how could Jonah have imagined he was going to flee from such a God by leaving the dry land and going off into the sea? Had Jonah forgotten the words of Psalm 139? "Whither shall I go from thy Spirit? Or whither shall I flee from thy presence?"

Jonah's rather pious "I fear the LORD" (1:9) seems a bit overblown, considering his disobedience and his attempt to get as far away as possible from Nineveh. Again his behavior is the opposite of what we might expect from one who claims to be such a God-fearing Hebrew. The only thing he fears is that the Ninevites might repent and that God might have mercy upon them.

When the sailors ask Jonah what they might do to appease his God, we are given a further surprise. Jonah responds: "Take me up and throw me into the sea; then the sea will quiet down for you" (1:12). Of course, Jonah could have offered to reconsider and go to Nineveh. But, no, Jonah would rather drown in the middle of the Mediterranean than preach to the Ninevites or see the Ninevites live and prosper.

Jonah's response is, in turn, in striking contrast to the pagan sailors' attitude toward Jonah. Jonah has now admitted that—all because of him—their cargo has been lost, their ship is about to be destroyed, and they may well lose their lives. Instead of being angry with Jonah and gladly throwing him in the sea, "the men rowed hard to bring the ship back to land" (1:13). In other words, the pious Hebrew Jonah, worshiper of the one God and Father of all, has no sense whatever of compassion for the pagan Ninevites; he simply wants them destroyed without warning. These pagan sailors, on the other hand, though they are about to lose everything because of the sins of Jonah, have compassion on Jonah and are willing to risk their lives to save him. "But they could not, for the sea grew more and more tempestuous against them" (1:13). Only after praying that God will not hold them accountable for acceding to Jonah's suggestion do they reluctantly throw him into the sea.

Immediately the storm subsides. And no sooner has Jonah sunk to the bottom than a great fish swims down and swallows Jonah. Worse, the fish swims right back toward the shore from which Jonah embarked. After three days and nights, and no doubt a severe case of indigestion, the fish "vomited out Jonah upon the dry land" (2:10). Thus God does not allow Jonah to flee from his presence or escape from his mission by committing suicide. Instead God provides a vehicle that transports Jonah directly, and despite the lack of a round-trip ticket, toward Nineveh. He is brought, kicking and screaming, back to his point of departure.

Playing with Words

Perhaps people today would better get the full comic effect of Jonah's foolishness if they imagined the story being told by Bill Cosby, after the fashion of his retelling the story of Noah and the flood. On the other hand, approaching the story from the standpoint of contemporary culture inevitably has its disadvantages. Certain details of the comic caricature of Jonah, for instance, are more apparent in the Hebrew. No doubt these allusions were clearer to the people who first heard or read the story.

The opening words of the book of Jonah are a case in point. "Now the word of the LORD came to Jonah the son of Amittai." Innocent as these words may seem, in Hebrew they contain two important allusions that are central to the comedy that is to follow. Jonah means "dove," a metaphor sometimes used for the people of Israel, as in Psalm 74:19. Now the image of the dove brings with it a trail of associations that—as the story indicates—are the opposite of what Jonah (Israel) really is.

The dove is associated with hope, as in Noah's sending out a dove to find land after the flood. Yet this dove (Jonah) behaves in a most contrary manner: sent out to warn of impending destruction, he refuses lest the judgment be averted. The dove is also associated with the theme of escape from troubles and evils, as in Psalm 55:6, "O that I had wings like a dove." Yet this dove (Jonah) tries to escape from his mission in the hope that Nineveh cannot possibly escape from doom. The dove is further associated with love, as in the Song of Solomon, in which the beloved is dovelike: "My love, my fair one . . . my dove" (2:13, 14). Yet this dove (Jonah) has not only no love for the Ninevites but not a penny's worth of sympathy or pity. Jonah is no dove at all; he is a hawk. Perhaps the only Hebraic association that is directly applicable to Jonah is that he is "like a dove, silly and without sense" (Hos. 7:11). Certainly, flightiness and silliness aptly describe Jonah's behavior throughout the story.

The other ironic allusion in the opening words is contained in the phrase "son of Amittai." Amittai means "faithfulness." A second contradiction with which the story is to deal is announced at the start. This "son of faithfulness" is completely disobedient. His response to the divine command is totally contrary to it. "Dove son of Faithfulness" flies off in the opposite direction lest he become the bearer of the least olive leaf of hope, love, and salvation.

The only other biblical context in which "Jonah son of Amittai" appears is equally significant to the story. The Jonah of 2 Kings 14:25 prophesies during the reign of Jeroboam, son of Joash, who is classified as a very wicked king and who "did what was evil in the sight of the LORD; he did not depart from all the sins of Jeroboam the son of Nebat, which he made Israel to sin" (vs. 24). Yet despite the wicked-

ness of Jeroboam, God, in his mercy, decides that he will not "blot out
the name of Israel from under heaven, so he saved them by the hand of
Jeroboam" (vs. 27). The theme of salvation in spite of great evil, along
with the literal meaning of "Jonah son of Amittai," made the associations surrounding the name of Jonah especially useful in developing a
comic parable.

Another comic device in the book of Jonah is the juxtaposition of
the imagery of rising and falling. The command given to Jonah is
"Arise, go to Nineveh" (1:2). Jonah's immediate response is to rise
but "to flee to Tarshish." This fleeing is then described in a succession
of *descents*. Jonah "went down" to Joppa and boarded a ship. Once at
sea he had "gone down" into the hold of the ship, had "lain down,"
and had fallen into a deep sleep. The sailors who were desperately trying to save the ship, when they found him, commanded him to "arise"
and call upon his God. When they cast (down) lots to determine who
was the cause of their situation, the lot "fell upon Jonah." Rather than
repent and offer to rise up and go to Nineveh, Jonah volunteered to be
thrown into the sea and therefore go down in death to Sheol. Literally
and figuratively, Jonah, to avoid rising up to go to Nineveh, went
down, down, down, down. Yet, no matter how low Jonah stooped or
to what depths he sank in his disobedience, God saved Jonah from destruction, just as God later saved Nineveh from destruction—with the
one difference that Nineveh repented; Jonah did not. We can imagine
him muttering as the great fish snatches him up and transports him back
in the direction of Nineveh, "Curses, foiled again."

Actually, what Jonah is said to have muttered during his three days
in the stomach of the great fish is a long prayer. The prayer seems so
out of character for Jonah and so eloquent for its gastric setting that
some interpreters have suggested that it is probably a later addition.
The prayer, however, repeats the theme of descent in chapter 1 in a
long cascade of imagery:

> "Out of the belly of Sheol I cried,
>   and thou didst hear my voice.
> For thou didst cast me into the deep,
>   into the heart of the seas,
>   and the flood was round about me;
> all thy waves and thy billows
>   passed over me. . . .

> The waters closed in over me,
>   the deep was round about me;
> weeds were wrapped about my head
>   at the roots of the mountains.
> I went down to the land
>   whose bars closed upon me for ever. . . ."
> (Jonah 2: 2–6)

In other words, to put it less poetically, Jonah dropped to the bottom like a stone!

The prayer itself sounds exemplary in its piety and suggests that Jonah has undergone a dramatic conversion. On closer examination, however, it is the prayer of someone who has turned to God in his extremity and as a last resort. Pious phrases, grand promises, and sacred vows easily pour forth from the soul in desperate circumstances. As John Holbert has suggested, Jonah's words are typical of what we might call "fox-hole" religion, or in this case "fish-belly" religion.[3] There is some question about the extent of the transformation.

Although Jonah acknowledges that God has rescued him from certain death by preparing a fish to dive down and swallow him, Jonah does not once acknowledge any guilt or evildoing on his part. He neither confesses nor repents. In fact, while offering thanksgiving to God for deliverance—"thou didst bring up my life from the Pit" (2:6)—Jonah places all the blame for his predicament upon God. The prayer in chapter 2 thus continues the comic satire on the self-contradictions of Jonah's position and behavior. It was Jonah, not God and not even the pagan sailors, who proposed that he be thrown into the sea. Yet in the prayer Jonah blames it wholly upon God: "thou didst cast me into the deep. . . . Then I said, 'I am cast out from thy presence; how shall I again look upon thy holy temple?' " (2:3–4).

Jonah seems to have learned little about God's presence from the experience, for he still localizes God in Israel and imagines him in residence in the temple in Jerusalem. This is reaffirmed in verse 7, in which Jonah says, "my prayer came to thee, into thy holy temple." The theology of Psalm 139 has still not gotten through to Jonah: "If I make my bed in Sheol, thou art there! If I take the wings of the morning and dwell in the uttermost parts of the sea, even there thy hand shall lead me . . ." (vss. 8–9). Perhaps even more relevant would be the words of Amos 9:2–3:

"Though they dig into Sheol,
    from there shall my hand take them;
though they climb up to heaven,
    from there I will bring them down. . . .
and though they hide from my sight at the bottom of the sea,
    there I will command the serpent, and it shall bite them."

In this case the "serpent" is a great fish who has swallowed the bite whole and who by now has a bad case of indigestion and beaches itself. The juxtaposition of the last sentences of chapter 2 is especially humorous. No sooner does Jonah exclaim piously, "Deliverance belongs to the LORD!" than the fish throws up! "It vomited out Jonah upon the dry land" (2:9, 10). At last the long downward spiral of descent is reversed. He now very literally *comes up* from the depths of the sea and is *thrown up* from the belly of the fish. Surely it is the most humiliating and undignified example of salvation in the Bible.

Comic Exaggeration and Understatement

"Then the word of the LORD came to Jonah the second time, saying, 'Arise, go to Nineveh, that great city, and proclaim to it the message that I tell you' " (3:1–2). This time Jonah is somewhat more receptive. Having spent three days swimming in the stomach of the fish and having been summarily disgorged on the beach, he is in what we might call a weakened condition. His spirit, though not willing, has been broken and his flesh is weak. He may be going under protest and he may still be of the opinion that God dwells primarily in Israel, but he knows at least that he cannot escape the long arm of the law. God's dominion, if not his presence, is extensive. "So Jonah arose and went to Nineveh" (3:3).

Nineveh is now described as "an exceedingly great city, three days' journey in breadth." We come here to an exaggeration that further accentuates the message and the moral of the author's satire. Since a day's journey was a unit of measure roughly equivalent to 20 miles, this would mean that Nineveh was 60 miles across. As everyone would have known, no cities in the ancient world were 60 miles across. In fact, the city of Nineveh has been excavated, and the dimensions of this walled metropolis were approximately 3 miles by 1 1/2 miles. The exaggeration is intended for comic and satirical effect—to heighten and dramatize the absurdities in Jonah's position. Indeed, the word *great* is used fourteen times in the book of Jonah, as compared with an average of only two times in the eleven other minor prophets. Throughout the story we are deluged with successive waves of hyperbole: great wind, great storm, great fear, great fish, great city, great cry, great evil, great conversion, great anger, great joy—beyond all of which is the greatness of God's steadfast love, mercy, and grace.

Overstatement and understatement are two of the most common devices used in jokes and comedies, and both are used repeatedly in this part of the story to make Jonah's behavior even more ludicrous. We are given the image of a vast city with a vast population. Then we are told that Jonah only goes into the city a day's journey, utters his message, and leaves. This contrasts the overstatement concerning size and population with several understatements. Jonah doesn't go throughout the city, giving his warnings. He doesn't even go to the center of the city, nor did he go to the king's palace from which the message might have been more quickly disseminated. In other words, he is making the most minimal effort. He has agreed, grudgingly and under duress, to preach to the Ninevites, but he has hardly put his heart and soul into it. He is going to do as little as he can get away with.

This juxtaposition of overstatement and understatement is carried further: Jonah not only makes no attempt to ensure that his message is heard by more than a handful of passersby. He also delivers the shortest message possible (only five words in Hebrew): "Yet forty days, and Nineveh shall be overthrown!" (3:4). There is no reference to who or why, no reading of charges, no invitation to repent, no attempt at persuasion, just an announcement of the demise of Nineveh.

The story then returns abruptly to overstatement. The result of this Lilliputian effort, perfunctorily delivered, is that the entire 60 mile wide city is converted. The world's shortest and poorest sermon becomes the world's most successful sermon. "And the people of Nineveh believed God; they proclaimed a fast, and put on sackcloth, from the greatest of them to the least of them" (3:5). Even the king—to whom, if to anyone, the message should have been delivered—when the tidings reached him also put on sackcloth and ashes and proclaimed a fast and a time of penitence. "Let man and beast be covered with sackcloth, and let them cry mightily to God; yea, let everyone turn from his evil way and from the violence which is in his hands'' (3:8). As a result of this mass display of contrition, God decides not to destroy the city.

And what is Jonah's reaction to this incredible evangelistic success, unparalleled in the annals of preaching, either before or after? What is the response of one who was more successful by far than Amos, Isaiah, Jeremiah, or all the prophets put together? "It displeased Jonah exceedingly, and he was angry" (4:1). Indeed, Jonah's reaction is even more opposite than this. He would rather die than witness God's mercy and pardon bestowed on the Ninevites. "Now, O LORD, take my life from me, I beseech thee, for it is better for me to die than to live" (4:3).

Jonah finally reveals the true motives behind his peculiar behavior throughout the story. He has long known that God is a God of love as well as wrath. Has not Israel many times been a recipient of divine forgiveness and restoration? He has feared all along that if he should warn Nineveh of an impending judgment and they should repent and turn from their evil ways, God would also spare them. "Is not this what I said when I was yet in my country? That is why I made haste to flee to Tarshish; for I knew that thou art a gracious God and merciful, slow to anger, and abounding in steadfast love, and repentest of evil" (4:2). The opening words of verse 2 are taken directly from Exodus 14:12, in which the Israelites were complaining about God's leading them out of the "security" of slavery in Egypt to the uncertainty of the wilderness. Jonah would rather stay within the false security of unredeemed vengeance and destruction than venture into the uncertain realm of mercy and forgiveness.

Jonah is now totally frustrated. We can picture him stomping out of the city, muttering, "I knew it, I knew it, I knew this was going to happen!" He then builds a booth for himself—a kind of grandstand seat—from which to "see what would become of the city." He is obviously still harboring the hope that God will change his mind once more and destroy the city. An 8.5 reading on the Richter scale will do just fine. Jonah is going to sit in his booth in the gleeful prospect of seeing the city go up in smoke, like Sodom and Gomorrah. This would finally make his trip worthwhile. (How many Americans have secretly, or openly, and for many of the same reasons, cherished the thought of dropping atomic bombs upon Moscow?)

The absurdities of Jonah's position come to a climax when God, wanting Jonah to be as comfortable as possible while he waits to witness the incineration of Nineveh, causes a large-leafed plant to grow over his head to shield him from the heat of the sun. "So Jonah was exceedingly glad because of the plant" (4:6). Note the comical way Jonah races back and forth between extreme elation and extreme depression, between exceeding gladness and exceeding anger, like an accelerated manic-depressive.

Then comes the lesson and the moral. While Jonah is comfortably lounging in the shade of the plant in eager anticipation of the death and destruction he hopes will be played out before him, God causes the plant to wither, exposing Jonah to the sun. To this God adds a wind off the desert, carrying biting dust and burning heat, causing Jonah to become faint and miserable just as he nears his moment of supreme triumph. Again—for the third time in the story—Jonah wishes to die: "It is better for me to die than to live" (4:8). "But God said to Jonah, 'Do you do well to be angry for the plant?' And he said, 'I do well to be angry, angry enough to die!' " (4:9). A perfectly healthy plant, which God has created, has been summarily destroyed.

Now we are given that marvelous punch line, which totally collapses Jonah's self-contradictory theology and behavior: "And the LORD said, 'You pity the plant, for which you did not labor, nor did you make it grow, which came into being in a night, and perished in a night. And should not I pity Nineveh, that great city, in which there are more than a hundred and twenty thousand persons who do not know their right hand from their left, and also much cattle?" (4:10–11).

Again overstatement and understatement accentuate the absurdity of Jonah's position. The figure of 120,000 infants ("persons who do not know their right hand from their left") suggests a total population of 1 million, which Jonah thinks nothing of seeing exterminated, though he is "angry enough to die" over the destruction of a plant. Furthermore, even if Jonah were justified in his vengefulness toward the accountable citizens of Nineveh, he could not be justified in the slaughter of 120,000 innocent children or the untold numbers of animals ("cattle" in the broad sense of domesticated animals in and around the city). Jonah himself has acknowledged this unwittingly in having such compassion on a single, innocent plant and in being outraged at its destruction. Perhaps if Jonah has no compassion for the citizens of Nineveh, he may have compassion for the host of innocents, and, if not for the innocents, perhaps at least for the cattle.

Yet Jonah is not justified in his attitude toward the accountable citizens of Nineveh either—as much as he has assumed the justice of his position throughout the story. Jonah has acknowledged that the God of Israel is a God of mercy and grace. How does he know this? Because Israel itself has many times been the recipient of unmerited forgiveness in the seasons of its own wickedness. The wording at this point in the story (3:10) is identical to that in Exodus 32:14, in which God forgives the Israelites after their idolatrous worship of the golden calf: "God repented of the evil which he had said he would do unto them" (3:10). Jonah, too, only days before had been the recipient of unmerited deliverance despite his own unfaithfulness and disobedience! If God should not spare Nineveh, why should he spare Israel or spare Jonah? On the other hand, if there is hope for Nineveh, with its great wickedness, there is hope for anyone.

The Punch Line

The satire has ended abruptly, without any resolution or moralizing, in fact very much as a humorous anecdote ends suddenly with the punch line. One either gets the point of the joke immediately or not at all—or perhaps, like the proverbial Englishman, a day later. The satire has ended with a question directed at Jonah, a question filled with great irony, a question that completely reverses the supposed wisdom of Jonah's sense of justice and the seeming foolishness of God's sense of compassion. Jonah's wisdom is reduced to foolishness, and God's foolishness is revealed as wisdom.

The question is not answered because it is the final punch line. It is not answered also because the reader or hearer of the story is invited to answer, to answer initially with a laughter that sees the foolishness of Jonah and acknowledges the wisdom of God. Yet, as in all great comedy, the butt of the laughter is not just the comic figure immediately before the audience, but the audience itself. The comic figure *repre-*

sents the audience, so the point of the joke has not been fully understood until this further step has been taken. The fool strikingly enacts the foolishness of our own hypocrisies and contradictions.

Who then is Jonah? He is, most immediately, the fellow Jew who displays Jonah's attitudes, perhaps justifiably so by ordinary canons of justice in view of the oppressions of the Assyrians and other conquering peoples throughout Jewish history. Such attitudes may also seem justifiable in the name of a divine status bestowed upon the children of the Abrahamic blessing and covenant. Yet, finally, all such justifications are without justification before the higher court and the larger wisdom of divine grace.

Ultimately Jonah is all of us, for all of us, individually and collectively, behave like Jonah at some time or another. We, too, have our good reasons for doing so. We, like Jonah, are inclined to believe that the kingdom of God operates primarily in our midst: within our nation, race, denomination, or political party. We are fairly confident that God is specially present among us and is less interested in and less available to other peoples. Surely he will show little mercy or forgiveness to our opponents and our enemies, nor should we. From our assured vantage point "Vengeance is mine, saith the LORD" is the last word relative to the unmistakably evil peoples, ideologies, and nations of the world. And just as certainly, *we* are the anointed instruments of divine vengeance.

From a literary standpoint the book of Jonah is a comic masterpiece, delightful but also devastating in its humor, irony, and satire. Through various comic devices it brings Jonah's beliefs and attitudes to a *reductio ad absurdum*. From a theological standpoint the book is to be ranked as one of the most thoroughgoing Old Testament statements of a universal religious vision. God, as the Creator of all, is the God of all places and peoples. There is nowhere that God is not present and available, no situation in which he cannot work and his voice cannot be heard, no place that is completely godless. At the same time, as Creator of all peoples, God is not only the God of Abraham, Isaac, and Jacob and their descendants, but the God of all nations. All are his children and, unlike unjust parents who spoil some of their children while ignoring or rejecting others, this God extends love and care to all.

Furthermore, not only can no one escape from the power and presence of God but this God is the God of grace and mercy. No one stands outside God's grace, just as no one stands outside God's presence. God—foolishly, from Jonah's perspective—pardons and delivers even those who are totally undeserving. Nineveh stands as the ultimate test of the divine capacity for unmerited grace. If even Nineveh can be spared, who cannot be forgiven?[1]

8

The Comic Vision in a Tragic World

Would that strife might perish from among gods and men!

—Homer,
The Iliad

In one of the earliest Laurel and Hardy films, *Big Business* (1927), Stan and Ollie are Christmas-tree salesmen in California, going from house to house in a Model T truck loaded with trees. The story begins innocently and enterprisingly enough, with a touch of the Christmas spirit and good cheer. Before long, however, they come to the door of a homeowner with a somewhat salty disposition who had just settled down in his easy chair with pipe, paper, and slippers. He is not interested in a tree.

Fair enough. But when the man shuts the door after declining a purchase, a tree branch gets caught in the jamb. Ollie rings for the irritated homeowner to open the door and release the branch. Then as Stan is explaining the reason for the further intrusion, the man slams the door and catches Stan's coat. Again the doorbell is rung, and as Stan is apologizing the incensed homeowner slams the door and once more catches the tree in the jamb. When the irate homeowner comes to the door this time, he brings along clippers, with which he cuts up the tree and tosses it on the lawn. Stan concludes, "I don't think he wants a tree."

Ollie, however, retaliates by pulling the doorbell and wires from the wall. When the dismayed homeowner picks up the phone to call the police, Ollie cuts the wire to the phone as well. The film then records a gradually escalating conflict in which the homeowner destroys their truck and trees, piece by piece, while Stan and Ollie destroy his house and shrubbery, piece by piece. "An eye for an eye and a tooth for a tooth" wins the day. What had started out with a "Merry Christmas" ends up with two piles of rubble.

Big Business offers a comic parable of an all-too-familiar situation between individuals, groups, and nations. It is the kind of situation that plagues marriages, neighborhood disputes, race relations, religious and political differences, and international clashes. Laurel and Hardy have depicted, in comic dress, the classical tragic situation in which two forces, each of which represents a certain good, collide and destroy each other. Two sets of values are in tension: the free enterprise system and the privacy of the home, the provider of goods and the consumer of goods. In the beginning both sides are well-meaning. Yet they end up devastating each other.

Tragic Irony

This story, as we are painfully aware, continues to be true in many places and in many ways. We do not have to look hard to see the tragic drama being played out again and again: Israeli versus Palestinian; Arab versus Jew; Lebanese Muslim versus Lebanese Christian; Iraqi Sunni versus Iranian Shi'ite; Irish Catholic versus Irish Protestant; Latin American rightist versus leftist; white Afrikaner versus black liberationist; East versus West German; North versus South Korean; Soviet Afghani versus Afghan rebel; Pakistani versus Indian; Sikh versus Hindu; and the list goes on. Though both sides view themselves as right and good and the opponent as wrong and evil, it is never as simple as either side would have it. If anything, the collision is usually between two sets of claims, both of which have some legitimacy but which become evils because of a refusal to admit any legitimacy to the opposing side. What is sought is not accommodation but victory.

Much of human history seems to be the history of tragic conflict, both in inspiration and result. In the twentieth century, however, given the escalating advances in science and technology, these tragic conflicts have become more and more deadly. Terrorism and militant fanaticism, as well, have become more potent forces than ever before. And the introduction of long-range missiles and nuclear armaments into the arsenals of contending superpowers has brought the whole of human history to the brink of an irreversible tragic finale.

When primitive peoples were limited to wielding clubs and throwing stones, the tragic possibilities were correspondingly limited. They could do only so much damage. The history of civilization is the history of increasing the scope and scale of the tragic. *Civilization* is a most ironic word in this context. We can now devastate not only whole cities but whole nations, perhaps all life as we know it. Never before has the tragic vision of human relationships been in greater need of challenge.

The comic vision has become both increasingly difficult and increasingly essential. As the humorist James Thurber once put it, "It is very hard to sustain humor, or the desire for humor, in a period when we seem to be trying, on the one hand, to invent a pill or a miracle drug that will cure us of everything, and on the other hand to invent machines for instant annihilation!" Hard though it may be, it is more imperative than ever that we understand and develop a comic perspective on ourselves and our relationships to others. The comic spirit is no longer a luxury for indulgence in lighter moments. It is not For Entertainment Only but a necessity if the prospect of greater holocausts is to be averted.

Comedians seem to have comprehended the folly of the tragic spirit better than most religious, political, and military leaders—better also than most tragedians. In one of Mark Twain's tall tales, for example, he tells how exercised he became about the considerable amount of discord among God's creatures and how he decided to experiment with the problem. He built a cage, and in it he put a dog and a cat.

> In an hour I taught a cat and a dog to be friends. . . . In another hour I taught them to be friends with a rabbit. In the course of two days I was able to add a fox, a goose, a squirrel and some doves. Finally a monkey. They lived together in peace; even affectionately.
>
> Next, in another cage I confined an Irish Catholic from Tipperary, and as soon as he seemed tame I added a Scotch Presbyterian from Aberdeen.

Next a Turk from Constantinople; a Greek Christian from Crete; an Armenian; a Methodist from the wilds of Arkansas; a Buddhist from China; a Brahman from Benares. Finally a Salvation Army Colonel from Wapping. Then I stayed away two whole days. When I came back to note the results . . . not a specimen [was] left alive.[1]

Historically, comedy has had a close relationship with tragedy, the two having developed almost simultaneously in ancient Greek theater. Within a few decades of the production of tragic plays in the theater of Dionysus, comedies began to be added for amusement. Yet comedies contained the seeds of more than amusement. They turned to some of the same issues as theatrical (and real-life) tragedies, but in a different manner and with a different spirit. Those differences represent the comic answer to tragedy. The emerging comic vision is offered as an alternative to the tragic vision and its tragic consequences.

One of the flaws in the tragic vision is that each side tends to absolutize itself and cling stubbornly to its position, regardless of the consequences to life and property. The truths and rights to which each makes claim are beyond qualification and compromise. Any differing claims must be resolutely denied. At best, superficial compromises may be made, as is commonly done when token privileges are granted in order to leave an unjust system fundamentally unchanged. Otherwise the tragic hero is willing to kill or be killed for "the principle of the thing."

When human beings lose all sense of the comic in relation to themselves, their convictions, and their suspicions, tragic collisions are inevitable. Only insofar as we learn to take our ideologies and beliefs less absolutely, our self-images less seriously, do we have a chance of softening tragic extremes and tragic extremism. If nothing else, people who have a refined sense of humor about themselves are less inclined to kill one another. They may even be more disposed to love one another.

A related problem that accompanies our deepest convictions is that their intensity easily translates into intolerance, aggression, hatred, and violence. Thus one of the terrible ironies of history is that *religion* has been among the primary sources of tragic conflict. As Pascal said, "Men never do evil so completely and cheerfully as when they do it from religious conviction."[2] While religious beliefs have been offered as the true basis for harmony and salvation, they have served equally well as a basis for alienation, hostility, and destruction. The same faith, hope, and love that would turn swords into plowshares and spears into pruning hooks seems as capable of turning them into swords and spears again.

Holy cities inspire not only pious pilgrims and prayers but holy wars. The gracious word of God serves as a vehicle for dispensing grace to ourselves and damnation to those who disagree with us. The very cross that symbolizes love, mercy, and forgiveness so easily becomes a banner under which to parade into battle and a crusading sword with which to smite heretics and crucify "infidels." The foot of the cross, in fact, has proven to be one of the best places to fight.

Similar ironies beset the radical enthusiast of whatever persuasion who, in fanatical certainty over the righteousness of a cause, zealously pursues some grand program or vision. Quasi-religious beliefs share the same tragic history as their religious counterparts. Nationalism, patriotism, racism, classism—isms in general—display the same inclination to absolutize themselves as do religious persuasions. Ideologies, whether social, political, or economic, have a high level of missionary and often military zeal but a low level of comic awareness.

In totalitarian countries those who turn their wit too visibly in the direction of the ascendant regime are open to the charge of unpatriotic, if not subversive, behavior. One can be jailed just as quickly for a humorous barb as for a clandestine plot. The French autocrat Charles de Gaulle once threatened a Parisian cartoonist, whose speciality happened to be caricaturing the French president, with imprisonment by invoking a law instituted in the time of Napoleon! In the Middle Ages the court jester who ridiculed the king walked a tightrope between hilarity and headlessness.

A common trait of rulers, revolutionaries, and not a few ecclesiastics is the unwillingness to laugh at themselves or to permit others to laugh at them. Laughter is perceived as a threat to the dignity and power of high office. To be sure, humor is amply used in such authoritarian contexts. We cannot do without humor entirely. But it is a humor reserved for those who deviate from the prevailing truths, laws, and dictates. In Stalinist Russia, for instance, comedies were permitted, even encouraged, by the government. Yet they were of a certain carefully censored type: comedies that targeted capitalistic countries and democratic values. This use of the comic simply reinforces the underlying tragic vision of life and its doctrinaire rigidity. We laugh at others as a way of justifying ourselves and our condemnation of those who disagree with us.

Only in the more liberal atmosphere, however modest, that emerged after the death of Stalin, were Russian humor and comedy permitted greater breathing room. The Soviet magazine *Krokodil* signaled the change shortly after Stalin's death in an unusual way, by running a full-page advertisement for the best political joke, anecdote, or satire of the year. After the minute details about the rules for entry, a line at the bottom of the page read: "FIRST PRIZE, FREE TRIP TO SIBERIA!"

Just as there is a correlation between the tragic vision and dogmatism, fanaticism, and oppression, so there is a connection between the comic vision and openness, tolerance, moderation, and freedom. When one is truly free, one is free to laugh. It is no coincidence that Pope John XXIII, who inspired and led the sweeping reforms in Vatican II and who brought such a conciliatory and liberating spirit to the papacy, was also gifted with a great sense of humor.

Warrior Virtues

Unfortunately, tragic values as well as tragic claims have dominated most of civilized history. A major strength of the tragic spirit has also been its greatest weakness, namely, its exaltation of warrior virtues: courage, loyalty, duty, honor, pride, indomitable will, unquestioning obedience, stubborn determination, passionate involvement, uncompromising dedication. How brave and wholesome and right these virtues have sounded to us! How noble, as the Greeks would put it! How much they have inspired our poetry and drama, our literature and songs, our sense of patriotism and religious fervor! Yet these same noble virtues have so often led directly or indirectly to all manner of evil.

Tragic heroism sees the world as a battlefield of contending forces: good against evil, truth against error, light against darkness, or simply us against them. Such a vision of life easily becomes a self-fulfilling prophecy. In the tragic mentality, positions are reduced to polar opposites—either/or, black/white, friend/foe. The tragic mentality has a deep suspicion of both/and, shades of gray, and calls for moderation. Attempts at steering a middle course are seen as inconsistent, confused, wishy-washy, or treasonous. To both sides in a tragic confrontation the advocate of temperance and accommodation is a traitor.

From the tragic perspective, human differences are automatically read as conflict situations, requiring a defeat of the enemy and a fight to the death. *All* differences are subject to this reading: Protestant/Catholic, Democrat/Republican, labor/management, feminist/chauvinist, conservative/liberal, theist/humanist, fundamentalist/modernist, creationist/evolutionist, and the list goes on. On this basis any two forces that find themselves at odds—whether capitalist and communist or homeowner and tree salesperson—are placed from the start on an irreconcilable collision course whose end can only be a mutual attempt at destruction. The greatest irony is that the one thing all opposing forces have agreed upon is the tragic vision of life, with its tragic virtues and tragic consequences!

In comedy, on the other hand, these military virtues are counterbalanced by another set of virtues. And what an odd collection of virtues: laughter, humor, playfulness, childlikeness, meekness, humility, flexibility, moderation, magnanimity, willingness to compromise, love. This love, in fact, is the highest form of love. It is not the love of which Jesus spoke when he said, "If you love those that love you, what reward have you? Do not even the tax collectors do the same?" (Matt. 5:46). Such love is the limit of love in the tragic setting; it is the love among friends of like mind. The love that Jesus taught is a love that reaches beyond this, even to one's adversary. "You have heard that it was said, 'You shall love your neighbor and hate your enemy.' But I say unto you, Love your enemies and pray for those who persecute you" (Matt. 5:43–44). The former advice is tragic; the latter is comic.

The comic virtues, from laughter to love, are made plausible and possible because they embody a greater appreciation for the muddiness of human nature and the ambiguities of human truth and goodness. People and circumstances are not so neatly divisible into black and white as tragic heroism would suggest as a basis for its inflexible stand.

Comedy mixes and confounds all rigid categories and fixed identities—much as Charlie Chaplin did for so many years with a tramp figure who was both an aristocrat and a gutter bum. Most of Chaplin's comedies between 1915 and 1940 played with the theme of confounding and uniting opposites. Charlie was both gentleman and tramp, rich and poor, beauty and beast, policeman and thief, even (in *The Great Dictator*) a Nazi dictator and a Jewish barber.

Chaplin's 1922 classic, *The Pilgrim*, is one of the finest examples of the comic impulse to break down the sharp distinctions that separate people from one another and pit one against the other. As the film begins, Charlie, an escaped convict, is running along a riverbank. There he chances upon the garb of a clergyman who has shed his clothes to take a swim. Charlie quickly exchanges his prison stripes for the clerical dress. In one of the pockets Charlie finds money, which he uses to board a westbound train. When the train arrives at a small town near the Mexican border, the convict/clergyman gets off only to find a church congregation awaiting the arrival of its new minister. They insist on taking him directly to the church and having him lead a service. Charlie does his best to play the parson's role but is none too familiar with religious services. Recalling the story of David and Goliath from his early youth, he pantomimes it in place of the scripture lesson, raising not a few eyebrows. His other identity betrays him, however, when it comes to the offering. While the ushers are taking up the collection, he has nothing to do, so he pulls up a chair, sits down, crosses his legs, and lights a cigarette!

Once Charlie's double identity is discovered, the local sheriff gives him the choice of returning to prison or going to Mexico. He chooses Mexico, but no sooner does he cross the border than he finds himself in the middle of a shoot-out between rival gangs. He runs back across the border, but there stands the sheriff. The film ends with Charlie, the convict/clergyman, running along the border, hopping back and forth between Mexican lawlessness and American law and order, a citizen of the no-man's land between the two.

In the comic vision the sharp lines we like to draw between ourselves and others are blurred. Instead a common humanity and a more all-encompassing perspective comes into focus. The comic hero occupies a kind of no-man's land between competing forces, a border region where both sides may come together in peace as well as conflict. If to tragedy belong the law court and the battlefield, to comedy belong the bargaining table and the diplomatic pouch. This is something of the same logic that finds the best mediators in those not completely identifiable with either side—as in the recent case of Philip Habib, United States mediator between the Israelis, Palestinians, Muslims, and Christians in Lebanon, who is a Christian Arab from Lebanon, raised in a Jewish neighborhood in New York City!

Comedy is usually seen as a cheap second to the sublime heights and stirring heroics of tragedy. Yet comic heroes display a distinctively different and more difficult heroism than tragic heroes. Fighting or retaliating is often easier than turning the other cheek or offering a conciliatory gesture. Willingness to yield or extend trust and friendship demands a larger spirit than tragic nobility. This does not mean that comedy is associated with cowardice but rather with magnanimity. As Mahatma Gandhi argued with respect to his doctrine of nonviolent resistance, it is possible to speak of a cat as refraining from killing a mouse, but "a mouse cannot be commonly said to refrain from hurting a cat."[3] For Gandhi, as for Jesus, meekness and humility are not to be confused with mousiness. They represent a higher form of character and strength.

The comic figure stands bravely between competing principles and forces in defense of those who would be trampled underfoot by either side. For comic heroism, persons are more important than principles, life and limb than abstract ideas, hungry people than sabbath laws. The comic hero is less inclined to sacrifice flesh and blood to bloodless ideals or bloody honor. Saving lives is more important than saving face. Sometimes the reward for such efforts is a truce, a peaceful coexistence, perhaps even a reconciliation. Sometimes the reward is being set upon by both sides, as Jesus was crucified by conquering Romans and conquered Jews.

Comic Reconciliation

Interestingly, the earliest form of tragedy in the Greek theater was not tragic in the sense in which we have long since come to use the word. Early tragedies began with a collision of forces that was *poten-*

tially tragic but that was averted by accommodation and reconciliation. The first two acts in a tragedy depicted two "worlds in conflict"—in Greek, *agon*. Then after presenting the legitimate values and claims of the prot*agon*ists and ant*agon*ists, and *agon*izing over the dilemmas involved, the conflict was resolved in the final act. The tragedy ended, not in death and destruction, but in averting disaster.

The Promethean trilogy of Aeschylus is especially instructive. In the first play (*Prometheus Bound*) Prometheus, uncompromising and unrepentant, presents his case for the theft of the sacred fire from Mount Olympus. Unfortunately, only fragments of the second and third plays have survived, but from what is known the second play would have taken up the case of Zeus and the gods equally vigorously. Then the third play, *Prometheus Unbound*, would have worked out an accommodation that satisfied both sides. In the Greek theater of the time, this happy conclusion would have been followed by a humorous satyr play and a comedy. The satyr play and the comedy celebrated, as it were, the reconciliation of the adversaries and the relaxation of the tensions built up in the first two plays.

After the time of Aeschylus, however, Greek tragedians began to portray conflicts for which there seemed to be no natural resolution. Instead the *deus ex machina* was introduced. As in the works of Euripides, in the third play a god or goddess was lowered to the stage in a basket. The divinity arbitrarily sorted things out, somewhat like a modern federal mediator in a labor-management dispute. Though the resolution was a bit artificial, it was nevertheless a resolution.

By the time of Sophocles, however, conflicts were being proposed for which no resolutions were even imagined. Instead, as in Sophocles' *Antigone* and *Oedipus Rex*, conflicts were simply presented in their unredeemed and unredeemable agony. Opposite values and principles were absolute and could not be qualified. Opposing sides in a dispute were totally uncompromising. This inflexibility was further reinforced by viewing the circumstances as determined by an inexorable fate. The only noble course was to see the conflict through to its bitter end.

Western civilization seems to have been determined, if not destined, to read human discord in the same way ever since. Considerable inspiration has arisen from rehearsing the tragic virtues of pride, loyalty, honor, duty, and unrelenting resolve. Even a cathartic pleasure has been derived from reenacting the inevitable fate of such noble in-transigence. From the dramas of Sophocles to Shakespeare's *Hamlet* and *King Lear* and Sartre's *Nausea* and *No Exit*, all have been destined to come to inescapable ends, descending, however grandly and nobly, into the regions of darkness, death, destruction, and despair. Hence the dictum in literature that comedies end in weddings; tragedies end in funerals. If we take Shakespeare's plays as a measure, *As You Like It* ends in multiple weddings; *Hamlet* ends in multiple funerals.

Early Greek tragedy was tragic in its beginning but not in its ending. The tragic conflict was not permitted to carry through to mutual destruction. Energies were moved toward a truce rather than a battle. Once the tragedians, such as Sophocles, offered dramas that were tragic both in beginning and in ending, it fell to the writers of comedy to do more than celebrate a reconciliation. Somehow they had to lead the way in bringing it about. Thus emerged the comedians, who de-bunked tragic extremism and its unbending virtues and who proposed comic solutions to tragic impasses.

Aristophanes, for example, suggests a charming comic compromise in his play *Lysistrata*. Two cities have been involved in interminable warfare against each other—an obvious reference to the long-standing hostilities between Athens and Sparta, and no doubt one of the reasons the tragic view of life was so natural to the Greeks. The women of both cities have grown weary of their husbands or lovers always leaving for the battlefield. The ordinary pleasures of life are constantly being for-saken for the intangible ideals of patriotic duty and the honor of the city. Endless waves of soldiers have been maimed or killed in the name of loyalty, pride, courage, perseverance, and the like.

So, led by Lysistrata, the women organize a "sex-strike." They deliver to both sides an ultimatum of their own for unconditional sur-render. No more bag lunches will be packed and no more sexual favors will be forthcoming until the men abandon their foolish flag-waving, their vain bravado and heroic talk. At first the men determine to stick it out. They refuse to be intimidated by women and women's threats. The result, however, is that the men of both sides give up and go home. "Make love, not war" wins the day. And life is returned to the simple pursuits of wife, children, job, friends, and housekeeping. These, it is realized, are the people and things most important after all.

In modern form the comic credo has perhaps never been stated more succinctly than by Chaplin at the end of his last "silent" film, *The Great Dictator* (1940). As a refugee Jewish barber fleeing toward the Austrian border, Charlie has been mistaken for his look-alike, the German dictator. He is speedily chauffeured to a nearby Nazi rally where *Der Führer* has been scheduled to speak. Hesitantly and haltingly, he begins (it is the first time that Chaplin has ever spoken in a film).

> I'm sorry, but I don't want to be an emperor. That's not my business. I don't want to rule or conquer anyone. I should like to help everyone—if possible—Jew, Gentile, black men, white. We all want to help one another. Human beings are like that. We want to live by each other's happiness—not by each other's misery. We don't want to hate and despise one another. In this world there is room for everyone. And the good earth is rich and can provide for everyone.[4]

Essentially, and at its best, this is the comic gospel. It is a foolish gospel, to be sure, for human beings are not always like that, probably not even on average like that. It is a foolish gospel, too, considering the tragic enormities of which "man's inhumanity to man" have been capable. Yet in its foolishness it represents a higher wisdom, a divine wisdom. It is, finally, the only way.[5]

Notes

Prologue: Divining the Comedy

1. Conrad Hyers, *The Comic Vision and the Christian Faith: A Celebration of Life and Laughter* (New York: Pilgrim Press, 1981).
2. See Elton Trueblood, *The Humor of Christ* (San Francisco: Harper & Row, 1964).
3. For a discussion of the range of comic elements in the Bible—humor, irony, sarcasm, satire—see Edwin M. Good, *Irony in the Old Testament* (Philadelphia: Westminster, 1965). Cf. Paul D. Duke, *Irony in the Fourth Gospel* (Atlanta: John Knox, 1985).
4. Quoted in E. T. Eberhardt, *In the Presence of Humor* (Salem, Ore.: Pilgrim House, 1984), p. 2.

1. The Humor of God

1. Reinhold Niebuhr, "Humour and Faith," *Discerning the Signs of the Times: Sermons for Today and Tomorrow* (London: SCM Press, 1946), p. 115.
2. Friedrich Nietzsche, *Thus Spake Zarathustra*, trans. Thomas Common (New York: Random House, Modern Library, n.d.), pp. 40–41.
3. C. S. Lewis, *The Screwtape Letters*, rev. ed. (New York: Macmillan, 1982), p. ix.
4. *Des cris de Paris*, quoted in Barbara Swain, *Fools and Folly During the Middle Ages and Renaissance* (New York: Columbia University Press, 1932), p. 219 n. 42.
5. C. S. Lewis, *The Magician's Nephew* (New York: Macmillan, 1955), p. 106.

6. Joseph Campbell, *The Masks of God*, vol. 1, *Primitive Mythology* (New York: Viking, 1959), p. 40.
7. Nietzsche, *Zarathustra*, p. 40.
8. Alan W. Watts, *Behold the Spirit: A Study in the Necessity of Mystical Religion* (New York: Pantheon, 1947), p. 179.
9. Paul M. Zall, ed., *Mark Twain Laughing: Humorous Anecdotes by and about Samuel L. Clemens* (Knoxville: University of Tennessee Press, 1985), p. 144.

2. Easter Hilarity

1. Conrad Hyers, ed., *Holy Laughter: Essays on Religion in the Comic Perspective* (New York: Seabury, 1969), p. 255. For the full text, see pp. 252–62.
2. *Commentary on Matthew*, Homily 6, 6, quoted in Hyers, *Holy Laughter*, p. 192.
3. Northrop Frye, "The Argument of Comedy," in *Theories of Comedy*, ed. Paul Lauter (Garden City, N.Y.: Doubleday, Anchor, 1964), p. 455.
4. Francis MacDonald Cornford, *The Origin of Attic Comedy* (London: Edward Arnold, 1914).
5. Wylie Sypher, ed., *Comedy* (Garden City, N.Y.: Doubleday, 1956), p. 220.
6. E.g., the recent issue of *Semeia* (no. 32), entitled *Tragedy and Comedy in the Bible*, ed. J. Cheryl Exum (Decatur, Ga.: Scholars Press, 1984), pp. 5–148, where the definition of comedy is narrowed to the stories that have an upturning movement and a happy ending. See my critique of such a view in "A Happy Ending of Sorts—The Underdog," in *The Comic Vision and the Christian Faith*, pp. 154–68.
7. See William Whedbee, "The Comedy of Job," *Semeia* 7 (1977):1–39.

4. Mary Had a Little Lamb

1. *London Times Magazine* (December 1, 1985).
2. Robert Payne, *The Great God Pan* (New York: Hermitage House, 1952), p. 13.

5. The Blue Book of Social Usage

1. Emily Post, *Etiquette: "The Blue Book of Social Usage,"* new and enl. ed. (New York: Funk & Wagnalls, 1928), p. 255.
2. Peter De Vries, *The Mackeral Plaza* (Boston: Little, Brown, 1958), p. 7.
3. Walker Percy, *Love in the Ruins* (New York: Farrar, Straus & Giroux, 1971).
4. Quoted in William Barclay, *The Beatitudes and the Lord's Prayer for Everyman* (New York: Harper & Row, 1968), pp. 223–24.
5. Sóren Kierkegaard, *Concluding Unscientific Postscript*, trans. David F.

Swenson and Walter Lowrie (Princeton: Princeton University Press, 1941), pp. 487–89.

6. Northrop Frye, *The Anatomy of Criticism: Four Essays* (Princeton: Princeton University Press, 1957), p. 166.

6. Miracles in Common Places

1. George Bernard Shaw, *Saint Joan* (Indianapolis, Ind.: Bobbs-Merrill, 1971), p. 113.
2. "The Estate of Marriage," 1522, in *Luther's Works*, vol. 45, *The Christian in Society II*, ed. Walther Brondt (Philadelphia: Muhlenberg Press, 1962), p. 39.
3. Conrad Hyers, *Zen and the Comic Spirit* (Philadelphia: Westminster, 1973), p. 92.

7. The Day Jonah Swallowed the Whale

1. For a detailed study of the literary form and usage in the book of Jonah, see Jonathan Magonet, *Form and Meaning: Studies in Literary Techniques in the Book of Jonah* (Frankfort: Peter Lang, 1976). For a theological interpretation, see Terence E. Fretheim, *The Message of Jonah* (Minneapolis: Augsburg Publishing House, 1977).
2. James D. Smart, "The Book of Jonah," in *The Interpreter's Bible* (Nashville: Abingdon, 1956), 6:871–75. For a recent discussion of Jonah as satire, which also alludes to its comic and humorous elements, see James S. Ackerman, "Satire and Symbolism in the Song of Jonah," *Traditions in Transformation: Turning Points in Biblical Faith*, ed. Baruch Halpern and Jon D. Levenson (Winona Lake, Ind.: Eisenbrauns, 1981), pp. 213–46. See also the study by John C. Holbert, "Satire in the Book of Jonah," *Journal for the Study of the Old Testament* 21 (1981): 59–81.
3. Holbert, "Satire," p. 73.

8. The Comic Vision in a Tragic World

1. Mark Twain, *Letters from the Earth*, ed. Bernard DeVoto (New York: Harper & Row, 1962), pp. 227–28.
2. Blaise Pascal, *Pensées*, trans. W. F. Trotter (New York: Random House, 1941), sec. xiv, no. 894.
3. Quoted in Erik H. Erickson, *Gandhi's Truth: On the Origins of Militant Non-Violence* (New York: Norton, 1969), p. 290.
4. Charles Chaplin, *My Autobiography* (New York: Simon & Schuster, 1964), p. 399.
5. For a fuller discussion of tragedy and comedy, see my development of their religious implications in *The Comic Vision and the Christian Faith*, chs. 5, 7, and 9.

Index of Scripture References

Index of Persons

Index of Subjects

(